MASTERCHEF
1992

MASTERCHEF 1992

FOREWORD BY LOYD GROSSMAN

GENERAL EDITOR: JANET ILLSLEY

EBURY PRESS
LONDON

First Published 1992 by Ebury Press
an imprint of the Random Century Group
Random Century House
20 Vauxhall Bridge Road
London SW1V 2SA

MasterChef 1992
A Union Pictures production for BBC TV Elstree
Series devised by Franc Roddam
Executive Producer: Bradley Adams
Producer and Director: Richard Bryan
Production Manager: Glynis Robertson
Production Co-ordinator: Sue Matthews

General Editor: Janet Illsley
Design: Clive Dorman
Front Cover Photograph: Helen Pask
Back Cover Photograph: Richard Farley
Food Photography: Gus Filgate
Home Economist: Kathy Man

A catalogue record for this book is available from
the British Library

ISBN 0 09 177376 8

Typeset by Clive Dorman & Co
Printed and bound in Great Britain by
Butler & Tanner Ltd., Frome and London

CONTENTS

FOREWORD

Time for another series of MasterChef. After months of form-filling, interviewing, shopping, chopping, stewing and grilling, twenty seven of the best amateur cooks in Britain fought their way through thirteen weeks of televised competition. At the end of it all, one of them – having performed in front of millions of viewers and under the scrutiny of the greatest chefs and most celebrated food lovers in the kingdom – emerged with the title MasterChef of Great Britain 1992. It is hard and sometimes heart-breaking work for our competitors. Why do they do it? There is always the thrill of the contest and perhaps most importantly the chance to share the very social art of cooking with the others – judges, fellow cooks and audience. It is also great fun and our cooks have uniformly praised the camaraderie and high spirits that run throughout the series. Cups of sugar are borrowed, hints on the sources and techniques are exchanged and lasting friendships have been formed. Why does Britain watch it? First because our long smothered national love affair with food is rising to the surface and secondly because of the powerful human drama of watching amateurs perform beautifully – what I call the "olympics factor."

Over the last three years the competition has evolved considerably: not necessarily in terms of kitchen skills which were always at a high level – but in terms of making progress with the way we prepare, serve and understand food. But what do we mean by progress? Let's begin with the elimination of anything that suggests that good food is dependent on overspending, pretentiousness or class. Good food is and should be for everyone, and the way to ensure that food makes its contribution to human happiness is to aim for simplicity, integrity, seasonality and respect for ingredients. More and more cooks are turning away from attempts to replicate hotel or restaurant food at home. They are coming to realise what ought to be self-evident truths: good food should taste good and look good with the minimum of fuss and fiddling. What looks good these days is food that looks like something edible not like something that ought to be hanging up in the National Gallery. What tastes good these days is food that has real flavour.

For MasterChef, 1992 was a year of bold and simple tastes: venison, wild mushrooms, guinea fowl, celeriac, chocolate and ginger all made centre stage appearances. Heavy, creamy sauces were rarely seen and the influence of ethnic cooking was more apparent than ever. Cooks are realizing that the time spent marketing and thinking is at least as important as time spent in the kitchen. As always my grateful thanks must go to Brad Adams and Franc Roddam for their inspired stewardship of MasterChef, to Richard Bryan who makes the programme work and look wonderful, to our judges for their hard work and good humour, and most important of all to every one of our contestants: each of them deserves a gold medal.

Loyd Grossman

NOTES FOR RECIPE USERS

Quantities are given in metric and imperial measures.
Follow one set of measurements only, not a combination,
because they are not interchangeable.

All spoon measures are level.

Fresh herbs are used unless otherwise stated.

INTRODUCTION

It seems almost inconceivable that another MasterChef year is over. We sent out more than two thousand application forms, tasted almost 350 dishes and travelled to the far reaches of the British Isles to unearth our twenty seven contestants who cooked their hearts out in the company of Loyd Grossman, his guests and our six cameras. And what a delightful and varied bunch our television finalists were: a sixteen year old student, a British Academy Award winning composer, a glamorous blonde police sergeant, an actor and a curate were amongst those who battled through the taxing regional 'cook-offs' and made their way to our Wembley studios to represent their regions in the programmes.

What amazing cooks they are! Each year all of us involved with the programme are astounded by the dramatic improvement in the overall standard of the dishes we taste. Our professional judges have been seen to cast many a nervous glance over their shoulders as they leave the studio!

So now it's up to you. Our judges have enjoyed every mouthful, and the crew have greedily polished off the remaining portions. We know how delicious these dishes can be, and can only hope that you and your friends will enjoy the menus and recipes in this book just as much as we have.

RICHARD BRYAN
Producer and Director
MasterChef

REGIONAL HEATS

THE NORTH WEST

VANESSA BINNS • ANNE MAY • ALAN SPEDDING

WINNER

VANESSA BINNS' MENU

STARTER

Little Cabbages of Wild Salmon with a Truffled Butter Sauce
"WONDERFULLY BUTTERY SAUCE" JULIA MCKENZIE
"REALLY SUCCULENT DISH" LOYD

MAIN COURSE

Duo of Tatton Park Venison
Butternut Pearls
Filo Pastry Tartlets of Celeriac Purée

DESSERT

Dark Chocolate Leaves layered with White Chocolate
Mousse in a pool of Vanilla Sauce

"GOOD TEXTURE. THE CONTRAST OF WHITE AND BROWN CHOCOLATE IS
GOOD" MICHEL ROUX

"QUITE BEAUTIFULLY BALANCED" JULIA MCKENZIE

V anessa lives in Cheshire with her husband,
16 year old daughter and two red setters which
she adores. She works every weekday morning at a prep
school, teaching kindergarten. Vanessa enjoys badminton
and tennis. She also collects paintings.

LITTLE CABBAGES OF WILD SALMON WITH A TRUFFLED BUTTER SAUCE

Court Bouillon:
600 ml (1 pint) dry white wine
1 carrot, roughly chopped
1 onion, quartered
1 clove garlic
thyme sprig
bay leaf
salt and freshly ground pepper

Cabbage:
1 green cabbage, about 600 g (1¼ lb)
200 g (7 oz) fresh wild salmon
50 g (2 oz) unsalted butter, melted

Sauce:
30 ml (2 tbsp) whipping cream
185 g (6 oz) unsalted butter, chilled and cut
    into small pieces
15 g (½ oz) truffle julienne
lemon juice to taste
freshly ground white pepper

To Garnish:
8 chervil sprigs

To prepare the court bouillon, put all the ingredients into a non-reactive saucepan, bring to the boil, then simmer for 20 minutes. Strain.

To prepare the cabbage, remove the outer leaves and take out the core. Put the cabbage in a large bowl with 30 ml (2 tsp) water, cover and microwave on high for 3 or 4 minutes to enable the leaves to be separated easily. Alternatively steam or boil for a few minutes to loosen the leaves. Place the cabbage leaves in a pan of boiling salted water and cook until tender, 3-4 minutes. Drain well and pat dry with absorbent kitchen paper.

Cut the salmon into slices. Place four 25 cm (10 inch) squares of muslin on your work surface. Brush melted butter over the inner surface of the cabbage leaves and season with salt and pepper.

Wrap a strip of salmon around a small leaf of cabbage to form a ball, then continue to build up a round about 5 cm (2 inches) in diameter, resembling a small cabbage, with the salmon slices and cabbage leaves. Pull up the corners of the muslin and secure tightly with string or tie together. Repeat to make 4.

Bring the court bouillon to a simmer in a large saucepan, setting aside 60 ml (4 tbsp) for the sauce. Add the 'cabbages' and cook for 5 to 10 minutes. Remove from the heat and keep in the cooking liquid until required.

Meanwhile, make the truffled butter sauce. Bring the 60 ml (4 tbsp) court bouillon to the boil in a saucepan, add the cream and boil for 2 minutes. Then add the butter in small pieces working on and off the heat to achieve a good emulsion, whisking continuously. Add the julienne of truffle and season to taste with lemon juice, salt and white pepper.

To serve, spoon the sauce on to individual serving plates and decorate with chervil leaves. Place a 'cabbage' on each plate and serve.

DUO OF TATTON PARK VENISON

700 g (1½ lb) fillet of venison
30 ml (2 tbsp) rich Madeira
salt and freshly ground black pepper
65 g (2½ oz) onion
30 ml (2 tbsp) vegetable oil
12 juniper berries, lightly crushed
250 ml (8 fl oz) good red wine
250 ml (8 fl oz) jellied venison stock
20 g (¾ oz) butter

Cut the venison fillet into two pieces. Choose the best piece and rub all over with the Madeira. Season well with black pepper and set aside to marinate. Cut the other piece of venison into 2.5 cm (1 inch) cubes. Chop the onion finely. Heat the oil in a flameproof casserole or heavy-based pan. Add the onion and cook until softened. Add the cubed venison and brown on all sides.

Put the juniper berries in a muslin bag and add to the pan with the red wine. Bring to the boil, cover and simmer gently until the meat is tender, about 1 hour. Take out the muslin bag and discard. Remove the meat with a slotted spoon and set aside. Add the stock to the pan and reduce by about two thirds. Return the meat to the pan, season with salt and pepper to taste and keep warm.

Heat the butter in a frying pan, add the marinated piece of venison and brown well on all sides. Transfer to a hot roasting dish and place in a preheated oven at 180°C (350°F) mark 4 for about 10-15 minutes to finish cooking.

To serve, slice the venison fillet thinly and arrange on a warmed serving plate. Spoon the venison in red wine sauce alongside.

BUTTERNUT PEARLS

200 g (7 oz) butternut squash
20 g (¾ oz) butter
5 ml (1 tsp) sugar
10 ml (2 tsp) lemon juice
pinch of salt

Cut the squash in half and scoop the flesh into small spheres, using a teaspoon or melon baller. Place in a saucepan with the butter, sugar, lemon juice and salt. Add sufficient water to just cover, then boil rapidly for about 10 minutes until the liquid evaporates and the butternut squash pearls are cooked and glazed; do not overcook. Serve immediately.

FILO PASTRY TARTLETS OF CELERIAC PURÉE

Celeriac Purée:
500 g (1 lb) celeriac
600 ml (1 pint) chicken stock
30 ml (2 tbsp) double cream
25 g (1 oz) butter
salt and freshly ground black pepper

Tartlets:
2 large sheets filo pastry
melted butter, for brushing

Peel the celeriac and cut into cubes. Cook in the chicken stock until tender, about 20 minutes.

Meanwhile, to make the tartlets, layer the two sheets of filo pastry together with melted butter. Cut into 4 squares. Lightly butter four 8 cm (3¼ inch) tartlet tins and line with the filo squares, gently pressing a 7.5 cm (3 inch) tartlet tin into each to hold the filo in place. Cook in a preheated oven at 200°C (400°F) mark 6 for about 10 minutes until golden brown, then remove from the tins.

Drain the cooked celeriac, reserving the liquid. Boil the cooking liquid until reduced to about 30 ml (2 tbsp) syrupy liquid. Put the celeriac and concentrated cooking liquid into a food processor or blender with the cream and butter, and work until smooth and light. Season with salt and black pepper to taste.

Fill the tartlet cases with the celeriac purée and serve immediately.

DARK CHOCOLATE LEAVES LAYERED WITH WHITE CHOCOLATE MOUSSE IN A POOL OF VANILLA SAUCE

White Chocolate Mousse:
1 gelatine leaf
240 g (8¼ oz) white chocolate
2 egg yolks
200 ml (7 fl oz) double cream, lightly whipped

Crème Anglaise:
250 ml (8 fl oz) milk
3 egg yolks
45 ml (3 tbsp) vanilla sugar

Chocolate Leaves:
125 g (4 oz) best quality dark chocolate

Chocolate Sauce:
45 ml (3 tbsp) milk
50 g (2 oz) dark chocolate, grated

To Decorate:
8 Cape gooseberries

To make the white chocolate mousse, soak the gelatine in a little cold water until soft. Meanwhile, grate the white chocolate into a bowl. Squeeze the excess water from the gelatine, then carefully melt it in 30 ml (2 tbsp) water. Pour the melted gelatine on to the chocolate and stir over a bowl of hot water until it has melted. Allow to cool, but not set. Mix the egg yolks into the cooled chocolate, then fold in the lightly whipped cream. Transfer to a suitable shallow rectangular dish and refrigerate until needed.

To make the crème anglaise, pour the milk into a saucepan and slowly bring to a simmer over a medium heat. In a bowl, whisk the egg yolks and vanilla sugar together until light and thick. Gradually whisk in half of the hot milk, then add to the remaining milk in the saucepan and mix well. Cook over a medium heat, stirring constantly, until the sauce thickens slightly. Do not allow to boil. Pour into a clean bowl and allow to cool.

To make the chocolate leaves, dampen a baking sheet with water and line it with non-stick baking parchment. Melt the chocolate in a bowl over a pan of hot water, then spread very thinly on the lined baking sheet. Allow to set, then cut into 4 cm (1½ inch) squares or shapes as desired.

To make the chocolate sauce for feathering, place the milk in a saucepan. Add the chocolate and bring to the boil, stirring constantly until the chocolate has melted and the sauce is smooth and shiny.

To serve, spoon the vanilla sauce on to serving plates and feather with the chocolate sauce. Layer the chocolate leaves with white mousse, then arrange in the centre of each plate. Place the Cape gooseberries decoratively to one side. Serve immediately.

REGIONAL HEATS
THE NORTH WEST

VANESSA BINNS • ANNE MAY • ALAN SPEDDING

ANNE MAY'S MENU

STARTER
Roquefort Tartlets served with a Walnut Salad
"WONDERFUL ALSO AS A MAIN COURSE FOR LUNCH" LOYD

MAIN COURSE
Guinea Fowl in an Orange and Chestnut Sauce
Potato and Kohlrabi Whirls
Sautéed Chestnuts
Broccoli Florets
"ON A SUNDAY IF ANYONE WERE TO GIVE ME THAT DISH I WOULD BE
EXTREMELY HAPPY" MICHEL ROUX

DESSERT
Pear Brandy Parfait served with a Pear and Raspberry Sauce
Almond Petits Fours
"TASTES EVEN BETTER THAN IT LOOKS" MICHEL ROUX
"COOL AND VERY REFRESHING" LOYD

Originally from France, Anne has travelled extensively and, since marrying, has settled in Cumbria. She qualified as a nurse in France and used to train students. Once she had mastered the English language, Anne joined a marine engineering company. She enjoys walking in the hills and making samplers to hang on her walls. Anne also has an impressive collection of Peruvian dolls.

ROQUEFORT TARTLETS WITH A WALNUT SALAD

Pastry:
120 g (4 oz) flour
pinch of salt
60 g (2½ oz) margarine, in pieces
25 ml (5 tsp) boiling water

Filling:
150 g (5 oz) Roquefort cheese
150 ml (¼ pint) double cream
1 large egg, lightly beaten
30 g (1 oz) walnuts, ground
freshly ground black pepper

Salad:
assorted salad leaves
15 ml (1 tbsp) wine vinegar
30 ml (2 tbsp) walnut oil
25 g (1 oz) walnuts

To make the pastry, put the flour, salt, margarine and boiling water into a bowl and mix together using a round-bladed knife. (Using boiling water will allow you to use the pastry immediately.) Roll out thinly and use to line 4 individual flan tins. Prick the bases with a fork.

Crumble the Roquefort into a bowl, add the cream and mix until smooth. Add the lightly beaten egg and the crushed walnuts. Add pepper. Pour the filling into the pastry cases and cook in a preheated oven at 190°C (375°F) mark 5 for about 45 minutes.

Meanwhile prepare the salad leaves. For the dressing, mix the vinegar with salt and pepper, then add the walnut oil and whisk to combine. Toss the salad leaves in the dressing.

Serve the tartlets just warm, with the salad. Garnish with the walnuts.

GUINEA FOWL IN AN ORANGE AND CHESTNUT SAUCE

4 guinea fowl joints, skinned
salt and freshly ground black pepper
30 ml (2 tbsp) oil
25 g (1 oz) butter
200 g (7 oz) button onions
200 ml (7 fl oz) stock
150 ml (¼ pint) white wine
finely pared rind and juice of 1 orange
15 ml (1 tbsp) redcurrant jelly
30 ml (2 tbsp) flour
425 g (15 oz) can unsweetened chestnuts,
    drained

Season the guinea fowl joints with salt and pepper. Heat the oil and half of the butter in a frying pan and add the guinea fowl joints. Turn until evenly browned, then transfer them to a casserole dish, using a slotted spoon.

Brown the button onions in the fat remaining in the frying pan, then add them to the casserole dish.

Mix together the stock, wine and orange juice. Add the redcurrant jelly and stir to dissolve. Gradually add this mixture to the flour, stirring to blend evenly.

Pour the stock mixture into the frying pan and cook stirring until thickened and smooth, then pour over the guinea fowl joints and onions. Add half of the chestnuts to the casserole with the orange rind, cut into strips. Adjust the seasoning and cook in a preheated oven at 180°C (350°F) mark 4 for about 1 hour.

Heat the remaining chestnuts slowly in the rest of the butter. Serve the guinea fowl in the sauce, garnished with the chestnuts and accompanied by the potato and kohlrabi whirls, and broccoli.

POTATO AND KOHLRABI WHIRLS

500 g (1 lb) potatoes
500 g (1 lb) kohlrabi
salt and pepper to taste

Cook the potatoes and kohlrabi together in boiling salted water until tender. Drain thoroughly and mash together until smooth. If the mix is too wet, stir in a pan over a low heat until dry. Add salt and pepper to taste. Pipe the mixture into whirls, about 5 cm (2 inches) in diameter, on a greased baking tray. Cook in a preheated oven at 180°C (350°F) mark 4 (with the casserole) for 20 minutes.

PEAR BRANDY PARFAIT WITH A RASPBERRY AND PEAR SAUCE

Parfait:
1 egg yolk
50 g (2 oz) icing sugar
250 ml (8 fl oz) double cream
50 ml (3½ tbsp) pear brandy (poire William eau-de-vie)

Sauce:
2 large flavourful ripe pears
30 ml (2 tbsp) raspberry jelly
15 ml (1 tbsp) pear brandy (poire William eau-de-vie)
icing sugar, to taste

To make the parfait, whisk the egg yolk and icing sugar together until pale and creamy. Beat the double cream to a Chantilly consistency, then fold into the whisked mixture with the pear brandy. Pour this mixture into a sorbetière and churn to a thick cream. Transfer to 4 ramekins and leave in the freezer for about 2 hours.

To make the sauce, peel and core the pears and place in a blender or food processor with the raspberry jelly and brandy. Blend to a smooth sauce. Taste, and if the sauce is a little too acid (depending on the pears), add icing sugar to sweeten.

To serve, carefully remove the parfaits from the ramekins and place on 4 cooled individual plates. Run the raspberry and pear sauce around each parfait. Serve with almond petits fours.

Note: If you do not have a sorbetière, freeze the mixture in a suitable shallow container for 1-2 hours until semi-frozen, then beat thoroughly to break down the ice crystals. Transfer to ramekins and freeze as above.

ALMOND PETITS FOURS

100 g (4 oz) ground almonds
60 g (2½ oz) caster sugar
15 ml (1 tbsp) apricot jam
1 egg white, lightly beaten
50 g (2 oz) slivered almonds
15 ml (1 tbsp) warm sugared milk

In a large bowl, mix together the ground almonds, sugar and apricot jam with enough lightly beaten egg white to obtain a firm mixture.

Transfer the mixture to a piping bag, fitted with a large fluted nozzle and pipe stars, about 3.5 cm (1½ inches) in diameter, on a greased baking tray. Using the remaining egg white, stick the slivered almonds on top.

Bake in a preheated oven at 220°C (425°F) mark 7 for about 10 minutes. Brush with the warm sugared milk, then transfer to a wire rack to cool.

REGIONAL HEATS
THE NORTH WEST
VANESSA BINNS • ANNE MAY • ALAN SPEDDING

ALAN SPEDDING'S MENU

STARTER
*Marinated Grilled Quail served with a Damson and Port Wine
Sauce garnished with Oyster Mushrooms*

MAIN COURSE
*Scallops and Prawns in a Ginger and Citrus
Butter Sauce served with Steamed Baby Vegetables
Seasonal Salad with a light Citrus Dressing*

"LIKE A BOUQUET OF FLOWERS. VERY VERY NICE, PERFECT SCALLOPS"
MICHEL ROUX

DESSERT
*Chocolate Marquise with Raspberry Coulis and Raspberry
Flavoured Crème Anglaise*

"THIS IS PERFECTION" MICHEL ROUX

"IT IS AS IF ALL THE CHOCOLATE IN THE WORLD WAS BOUGHT INTO THIS
DISH. I WOULD BE HAPPY TO BE SERVED IT ANYWHERE" LOYD

A lan is an electrician from Cleator Moor in Cumbria,
currently working under contract at the nuclear
processing plant in Sellafield. A keen photographer, Alan is
also a martial arts enthusiast and a karate black belt. At home,
Alan has an unusual collection – of piranha fish!

MARINATED GRILLED QUAIL served WITH A DAMSON AND PORT WINE SAUCE GARNISHED WITH OYSTER MUSHROOMS

4 plump fresh quail

Marinade:
60 ml (4 tbsp) white wine vinegar
60 ml (4 tbsp) Worcestershire sauce
30 ml (2 tbsp) hazelnut oil
30 ml (2 tbsp) lemon juice

Sauce:
150 ml (¼ pint) good rich chicken stock
5 ml (1 tsp) dried Provençal herbs
120 ml (4 fl oz) port
120 ml (4 fl oz) sherry
30 ml (2 tbsp) damson jelly
knob of butter
salt and freshly ground black pepper

To Garnish:
4 oyster mushrooms, sautéed in a little butter
French salad leaves, tossed in hazelnut oil
4 cherry tomatoes

Rinse the quail inside and out and pat dry with absorbent kitchen paper. Using scissors, cut down each side of the backbone, then remove. Using the palm of your hand, flatten the quail.

Combine the ingredients for the marinade in a shallow dish. Add the quail and leave to marinate in a cool place overnight.

To make the sauce, put the chicken stock, provençal herbs, port and sherry in a saucepan and simmer until reduced by about three-quarters. Add the damson jelly, stir and bring back to the boil. Stir in a small piece of butter to shine the sauce, then season to taste with salt and pepper.

Lift the quail out of the marinade. Cook the quail under a preheated grill for 6 minutes, basting with the marinade and turning halfway through cooking.

Spread the sauce over half of the plate and place the quail on the sauce. Dot the sautéed oyster mushrooms around the sauce. Garnish with the salad leaves and cherry tomatoes.

SCALLOPS AND PRAWNS IN A GINGER AND CITRUS BUTTER SAUCE SERVED WITH STEAMED BABY VEGETABLES

16 large scallops, shelled
20 large raw prawns, shelled and deveined
lemon juice to taste

Sauce:
5 cm (2 inch) piece fresh root ginger, peeled
    and sliced
170 ml (6 fl oz) Sauternes or other dessert
    wine
60 ml (4 tbsp) double cream
175 g (6 oz) unsalted butter, cubed
juice of ½ lemon
juice of ½ lime
salt and freshly ground black pepper

To Serve:
steamed baby vegetables, eg carrots,
    sweetcorn, courgettes, fine beans, cherry
    tomatoes

To Garnish:
dill sprigs
wild celery leaves
lemon and lime zest

First make the sauce. Put the sliced ginger and wine in a saucepan over gentle heat and allow to reduce very slowly, for about 30 minutes to about 15 ml (1 tbsp) syrup. Add the double cream and bring to the boil. Take off the heat and whisk in the butter cubes, two at a time. Strain, then add the citrus juices and seasoning to taste.

Cut each scallop in half and season with salt, pepper and lemon juice. Season the prawns with salt and pepper. Put the prawns into a steamer and gently steam for 2 minutes. Add the scallops and steam for 1 minute.

Remove the scallops and prawns from the steamer and arrange on heated serving plates. Pour over the sauce. Arrange the steamed baby vegetables on the plates, alternating colours for maximum effect.

Garnish with dill sprigs and dot with a few wild celery leaves. Sprinkle over a little lemon and lime zest.

CHOCOLATE MARQUISE WITH RASPBERRY COULIS AND RASPBERRY-FLAVOURED CRÈME ANGLAISE

Chocolate Mousse:
80 g (3 oz) dark chocolate
20 ml (1½ tbsp) instant coffee granules
6 egg yolks
125 g (4 oz) caster sugar
5 ml (1 tsp) honey
140 g (4½ oz) unsalted butter
80 g (3 oz) cocoa powder
225 ml (7½ fl oz) double cream

Crème Anglaise:
8 egg yolks
75 g (3 oz) caster sugar
600 ml (1 pint) full-cream milk
1 vanilla pod, split
30 ml (2 tbsp) framboise (raspberry liqueur)
   or kirsch

Raspberry Coulis:
300 g (10 oz) sugar
150 ml (¼ pint) water
700 g (1½ lb) raspberries
75 ml (5 tbsp) framboise (raspberry liqueur)
   or kirsch

To Decorate:
fresh raspberries
mint leaves

To make the chocolate mousse, melt the chocolate in a bowl over a pan of hot water. Dissolve the coffee in 20 ml (1½ tbsp) hot water. Mix together the melted chocolate, egg yolks, sugar, coffee and honey.

In another bowl, cream together the butter and cocoa powder, then mix with the chocolate mixture. Whip the double cream until it forms soft peaks, then fold into the chocolate mixture.

Brush individual moulds with butter, then line with cling film. Pour in the chocolate mixture and leave to set in the refrigerator.

To make the crème anglaise, whisk the egg yolks and sugar together in a bowl. Place the milk in a saucepan with the vanilla pod and bring slowly to the boil. Slowly pour the milk onto the egg and sugar mixture, stir well, then return to the pan and heat gently, stirring until thickened; do not boil. Remove the vanilla pod. Allow to cool.

To make the raspberry coulis, dissolve the sugar in the water in a saucepan over a low heat, then bring to the boil and boil for 1 minute to make a sugar syrup. Remove from the heat and while it is still hot, add the raspberries. Allow to cool then purée in a blender or food processor and sieve to remove pips. Add the liqueur.

Flavour the cooled crème anglaise with the liqueur and 30 ml (2 tbsp) of the raspberry coulis.

Unmould each marquise by dipping into hot water for 5 seconds, then carefully turning out on to individual serving plates. Pour a ring of raspberry coulis around the outside of each plate. Fill in with the raspberry crème anglaise, then feather with a chopstick. Decorate with raspberries and mint leaves to serve.

Regional Heats
The Midlands

Gregory Lewis • Vera Bloor • Jane O'Sullivan

Winner

Gregory Lewis' Menu

Starter

*Pan-fried Langoustines, Monkfish and Scallops with a
Spaghetti of Vegetables in Chive and Cinnamon Butter*

"Definitely Good. Very well thought out this dish – unusual"
Patrick Moore

Main Course

*Rack of Lamb in a Wine and Shallot Sauce
with Horseradish and Ginger Röstis
Seasonal Vegetables*

"A great combination" Loyd

Dessert

*Tropical Cream Dessert with Passion Fruit Coulis and a
Caramelised Pineapple Salad*

Greg, at 16 our youngest contestant, lives in Market
Bosworth, Warwickshire with his family and has just
taken nine GCSE's at Dixie Grammar School. In 1991 he was a
Future Cooks Finalist and in August he will start a highly
coveted apprenticeship under Michel Bourdin in the kitchens
of London's Connaught Hotel. Greg enjoys ten pin bowling
and is a keen cricketer.

PAN-FRIED LANGOUSTINES, MONKFISH AND SCALLOPS WITH A SPAGHETTI OF VEGETABLES IN CHIVE AND CINNAMON BUTTER

15 g (½ oz) unsalted butter
8-12 medallions of monkfish
8-12 peeled langoustines
4-6 shelled scallops
salt and freshly ground black pepper
squeeze of lemon juice

Spaghetti of Vegetables:
2 large carrots
3 outer leaves of a fennel bulb
2 medium courgettes
1 leek
a little sugar
knob of butter

Chive Butter:
2.5 ml (½ tsp) ground cinnamon
125 g (4 oz) cold unsalted butter, diced
30 ml (2 tbsp) chopped chives

To prepare the spaghetti of vegetables, trim the ends and rounded edges off the carrots. Cut into 3 mm (⅛ inch) slices, then cut into 3 mm (⅛ inch) strips to resemble spaghetti. Place in a saucepan with a little water, a little sugar and a knob of butter. Bring to the boil and simmer for about 4 minutes until cooked but firm. Drain, refresh in cold water and drain on absorbent kitchen paper.

Repeat with the fennel and courgettes, cutting into 3 mm (⅛ inch) strips and discarding the seeds of the courgettes, but add salt to the water instead of sugar. Cook the fennel for 5-6 minutes, the courgettes for about 2 minutes. Drain, refresh and drain. Trim the leek, halve and cut into julienne strips. Cook in boiling salted water for 1 minute. Drain, refresh and drain on absorbent kitchen paper.

To make the chive butter, heat 60 ml (4 tbsp) lightly salted water and the cinnamon in a small heavy pan over gentle heat. Whisk in the cold butter a little at a time until well incorporated. Add the chopped chives.

Meanwhile cook the fish. Melt the unsalted butter in a small frying pan until hot, but do not burn. Add the monkfish and toss for 1 minute, then add the langoustines and cook for a further 1 minute. Finally add the scallops, shake the pan and cook for about 30 seconds. Season with salt and pepper. Add a dash of lemon juice. Remove from the heat.

Place the prepared vegetables in a bowl and mix carefully with a fork. Add the warm chive butter and toss well. Using a slotted spoon, lift a portion onto each warmed serving plate. Add any remaining chive butter to the fish, shaking the pan. Carefully lift out the fish and arrange around the vegetables. Drizzle the chive butter remaining in the pan over the vegetables and fish. Serve immediately.

Note: Buy the smaller quantities of fish suggested if you wish to serve a small starter.

RACK OF LAMB IN A WINE AND SHALLOT SAUCE

The racks of lamb should be 'Frenched' – well trimmed and lean. Reserve any spare bones to make a trivet to roast the lamb on, or ask your butcher for a few extra bones.

2 racks of lamb, each with 6 chops
30 ml (2 tbsp) olive oil
2 rosemary sprigs
2 thyme sprigs
salt and freshly ground black pepper

Wine and Shallot Sauce:
8 shallots, roughly chopped
1 thyme sprig
1 bay leaf
50 ml (2 fl oz) port
50 ml (2 fl oz) matured sherry vinegar
400 ml (14 fl oz) red wine
400 ml (14 fl oz) lamb stock
15 g (½ oz) cold unsalted butter, diced

Leek Garnish:
1 leek
groundnut oil for frying

First prepare the wine and shallot sauce. Combine all the ingredients, except the stock and butter, in a bowl or non-reactive pan and leave to infuse as long as time allows, but preferably overnight. Transfer to a pan if necessary and bring to the boil. Simmer until reduced by two thirds. Add the stock and reduce again by half. Strain through a fine sieve and blend in the butter. Keep warm.

Heat the oil in a large frying pan until very hot. Sear each rack of lamb for 1 minute on each side and 3 minutes on its back. Transfer to a hot roasting tin, placing the rack on the reserved lamb bones. Lay a sprig of thyme and rosemary on each rack and roast in a preheated oven at 220°C (425°F) mark 7 for 12 minutes. Season.

To prepare the garnish, halve the leek and cut into fine julienne strips. Heat the oil to 140°C (285°F) and fry the leeks until pale golden in colour. Drain well on absorbent kitchen paper.

Leave the meat to rest in a warm place for a few minutes before carving into individual cutlets. Serve the cutlets on the horseradish and ginger röstis. Spoon the wine and shallot sauce around, and top with the leek garnish. Serve with a selection of baby vegetables.

HORSERADISH AND GINGER RÖSTIS

2.5 cm (1 inch) piece fresh root ginger, grated
25 g (1 oz) fresh horseradish, grated
2 large potatoes, peeled and grated
salt and freshly ground black pepper
125 g (4 oz) butter, melted

Put the grated ginger in a small saucepan, add water to cover, bring to the boil and simmer for 5 minutes. Drain, refresh in cold water; drain.

Put the grated potato in a clean tea-towel and squeeze out all the moisture. Turn into a large bowl and add the ginger and horseradish, salt and pepper. Carefully mix well with a fork to disperse the flavourings evenly. Stir in 45 ml (3 tbsp) melted butter.

Heat the remaining butter in a pan until foaming. Place a greased 10 cm (4 inch) muffin ring in the pan and fill with a quarter of the potato mixture. Press down well and remove the ring. Repeat to shape a further 3 rostis. Cook on one side for approximately 5 minutes until golden. Turn carefully and cook the other side. Drain on absorbent kitchen paper for a few seconds, then transfer to a wire rack to retain crispness. Reheat the röstis in a hot oven for a few minutes before serving.

TROPICAL CREAM DESSERT WITH PASSION FRUIT COULIS AND A CARAMELISED PINEAPPLE SALAD

I use the miniature Queen pineapples for this dessert as they have a delicious sweet flavour, but you could use one standard pineapple instead. The pineapple and sponge can be cooked at the same time.

3 Queen pineapples
25 g (1 oz) caster sugar (approximately)

Sponge Base:

1 egg white
30 g (1 oz) caster sugar
1 egg yolk
30 g (1 oz) plain flour, sifted
5 g (¼ oz) unsalted butter, melted

To Assemble:

45 ml (3 tbsp) Malibu or white rum
  (approximately)
150 ml (¼ pint) whipping cream
2 amaretti biscuits, crushed

Coulis:

12 passion fruit
juice of 1 large orange
65 g (2½ oz) caster sugar
50 ml (2 fl oz) water

Peel the pineapples and cut two of them into thin rings; remove the core and reserve four rings. Cut the remaining rings into small pieces. Line a baking sheet with non-stick baking parchment and butter liberally. Spread the pineapple pieces and the 4 pineapple rings on the baking sheet and sprinkle generously with sugar. Bake in a preheated hot oven at 220°C (425°F) mark 7 for about 8 minutes.

To make the sponge, line a baking sheet with non-stick baking parchment. Whisk the egg white to the soft peak stage, then gradually whisk in the sugar.

Whisk in the egg yolk, then fold in the sifted flour, followed by the melted butter. Spread evenly on the prepared baking sheet to a 1 cm (½ inch) thickness and bake for about 8 minutes until golden brown.

Transfer to a wire rack to cool. Slice the remaining pineapple and chop finely in a food processor. Drain on absorbent kitchen paper.

To assemble, lightly grease 4 stainless steel rings, 5 cm (2 inches) deep and 5 cm (2 inches) in diameter. Cut four circles of sponge to fit the base of the rings. Press a sponge base into each ring and sprinkle with Malibu or white rum. Whip the cream with 30 ml (2 tbsp) Malibu or white rum until stiff then fold in the finely chopped pineapple. Spoon into the rings, filling them to the top. Level off the surface. Open freeze for at least 1 hour. Transfer to the refrigerator 30 minutes before serving.

To make the coulis, halve the passion fruit and scoop out the seeds and pulp into a bowl. Strain the orange juice and add to the passion fruit with the sugar and water. Transfer to a blender or food processor and whizz for 20 seconds. Bring the passion fruit coulis to the boil, skim any froth from the surface and simmer for 2 minutes. Strain through a fine sieve and allow to cool.

To serve, cut four more sponge rings and use these to ease the tropical creams out of their moulds, then discard. Roll the sides of the tropical creams in crushed biscuits to coat, then place one in the centre of each serving plate. Surround each with passion fruit coulis and arrange the caramelised pineapple salad around the coulis. Top each tropical cream with a pineapple ring.

REGIONAL HEATS
THE MIDLANDS
GREGORY LEWIS • VERA BLOOR • JANE O'SULLIVAN

VERA BLOOR'S MENU

STARTER
*Wild Mushroom Goulash garnished with Puff Pastry Fleurons
and Seasonal Salad Leaves*

MAIN COURSE
*Fillet of Venison in a Damson Brandy Sauce
Filo Parcels of Spinach with Lemon, Nutmeg and Garlic
Garlic Potatoes*
"SPINACH AND VENISON ARE WONDERFUL TOGETHER" CAROLINE
WALDEGRAVE
"A GREAT SUCCESS" PATRICK MOORE

DESSERT
Apple Mille Feuille with Raspberry Sauce
"A GREAT LOOKING PUDDING" LOYD

Vera and her husband are both police sergeants living in
Staffordshire. She is now a Custody Officer dealing with
serious crime, and recently passed her Inspector's exams.
Absailing, weight training and aerobics keep Vera extremely
fit. By way of contrast, she enjoys making wedding cakes for
friends and relations.

WILD MUSHROOM GOULASH

45 ml (3 tbsp) olive oil
1 large clove garlic, finely chopped
2 shallots, finely chopped
500 g (1 lb 2 oz) wild mushrooms (an
  assorted mixture of those in season)
200 g (7 oz) tomato concasse (see note)
30 ml (2 tbsp) celeriac leaves, roughly
  chopped
salt and freshly ground black pepper
paprika

Fleurons:
50 g (2 oz) readymade puff pastry

To Serve:
salad leaves, tossed in a walnut-flavoured
  vinaigrette

First prepare the fleurons. Roll the pastry out thinly and cut into crescent shapes, about 5 cm (2 inches) long. Place on a greased baking tray and bake in a preheated oven at 220°C (425°F) mark 7 for about 5 minutes until crisp and golden brown.

Heat the oil in a frying pan, add the garlic and shallots and sweat for 2 minutes. Add the mushrooms, adding firmer varieties first, and sauté over high heat until they start to soften.

Add the tomato concasse and celeriac leaves. Season with salt, pepper and paprika. Warm through, then serve immediately, garnished with the puff pastry fleurons and salad.

Note: To prepare the tomato concasse, use about 350 g (12 oz) tomatoes. Plunge into boiling water for about 30 seconds, then remove and peel away the skins. Quarter the tomatoes, discard seeds, then finely chop the flesh. Use as tomato concasse.

FILLET OF VENISON IN A DAMSON BRANDY SAUCE

I use wild, young venison and my own homemade damson brandy for this recipe.

*4 venison fillets, each weighing about 175 g
  (6 oz)
15 ml (1 tbsp) olive oil*

Marinade:
*30 ml (2 tbsp) hazelnut oil
salt and freshly ground black pepper
fresh bouquet garni, eg sprigs of parsley,
  thyme, bay leaf
2 glasses good red wine
1 carrot, chopped
1 small onion, chopped
1 celery stick, chopped
3 juniper berries*

Sauce:
*450 ml (¾ pint) venison stock
225 g (8 oz) damsons
1 cinnamon stick
30 ml (2 tbsp) red wine vinegar
75 ml (3 fl oz) damson brandy
25 g (1 oz) chilled butter, diced*

Brush the venison fillets with the hazelnut oil, then season with salt and pepper. Place in a shallow container with all the other marinade ingredients, cover and leave to marinate for 1-2 hours. Meanwhile, simmer the venison stock in a saucepan until reduced by about half.

Set aside 8 damsons for garnish. Put the rest in a saucepan with the cinnamon stick and 15 ml (1 tbsp) water. Cook until quite soft. Discard the cinnamon and remove the damson stones. Purée the damsons in a blender or food processor, then pass through a sieve.

Heat the wine vinegar in a saucepan until it has almost evaporated, then add the stock, damson purée and damson brandy. Add the 8 reserved damson and heat through gently until softened; lift out with a slotted spoon, then carefully remove the stones, retaining the shape of the fruit. Reserve for garnish. Season the sauce and simmer until reduced and thick enough to coat the back of a spoon.

Remove the venison from the marinade and pat dry with absorbent kitchen paper. Reserve the marinade. Heat the oil in a frying pan and seal the venison for about 1 minute on each side. Transfer the venison to an ovenproof dish, pour over the marinade and cook in a preheated oven at 190°C (375°F) mark 5 for 10-12 minutes. Meanwhile, whisk the butter into the sauce, a piece at a time.

To serve, cut the venison into 1 cm (½ inch) thick medallions. Arrange in an overlapping circle on each serving plate. Spoon the sauce over the meat and garnish with the damsons.

Note: To make damson brandy, put 600 ml (1 pint) brandy, 450 g (1 lb) damsons and 225 g (8 oz) sugar in a sterilized wide-necked jar, seal and leave in a dark place for 8 weeks to mature. Strain off the fruit and eat separately. Bottle the damson brandy.

If damson brandy is unobtainable, substitute 75 ml (3 fl oz) brandy and 10 ml (2 tsp) brown sugar, and increase the quantity of damsons to 300 g (10 oz).

FILO PARCELS OF SPINACH WITH LEMON, NUTMEG AND GARLIC

700 g (1½ lb) fresh spinach, washed and
stalks removed
75 g (3 oz) unsalted butter
1 clove garlic, crushed
twelve 10 cm (4 inch) squares of filo pastry
50 g (2 oz) butter, melted
salt and freshly ground black pepper
5 ml (1 tsp) freshly grated nutmeg
7.5 ml (1½ tsp) lemon juice

Pat the spinach dry with absorbent kitchen paper. Melt the unsalted butter in a large deep pan with the garlic over a low heat, then add the spinach. Cover and cook over a moderate heat, stirring occasionally, for about 3-4 minutes until the spinach softens and wilts.

Brush 3 squares of filo pastry with melted butter and pile on top of each other, at an angle, to form a 'star' shape. Season the spinach with salt, pepper and nutmeg. Add the lemon juice. Place a heaped spoonful of spinach in the centre of the pastry star. Bring the corners up over the filling and scrunch together to form a parcel. Repeat to make another three parcels. Place on a lightly greased baking tray. Cover and refrigerate for 1 hour.

Bake the filo parcels in a preheated oven at 200°C (400°F) mark 6 for 10-15 minutes, until golden brown and crisp. Serve immediately.

GARLIC POTATOES

12 cloves garlic
4 potatoes, peeled
50 g (2 oz) butter
30 ml (2 tbsp) walnut oil
garlic salt, for sprinkling

Crush 8 garlic cloves; leave the rest whole. Using a melon baller, shape small potato balls, allowing 6-8 per person.

Blanch the potato balls in boiling salted water containing the whole garlic cloves, for about 1 minute. Drain thoroughly.

Melt the butter in an ovenproof dish, add the oil and crushed garlic. Add the potatoes, toss well and sprinkle with a little garlic salt.

Roast in a preheated oven at 190°C (375°F) mark 5 for about 30 minutes until tender with a crisp golden brown surface. Serve immediately.

APPLE MILLE FEUILLE WITH RASPBERRY SAUCE

3 large cooking apples
juice of 2 lemons
30 ml (2 tbsp) caster sugar (or to taste)
2 gelatine leaves

Crème Patissière:
2 egg yolks
50 g (2 oz) caster sugar
20 g (¾ oz) plain flour
300 ml (½ pint) milk
few drops of vanilla essence
300 ml (½ pint) double cream

Raspberry Sauce:
225 g (8 oz) raspberries
50 g (2 oz) caster sugar
90 ml (3 fl oz) water
squeeze of lemon juice (optional)

To Glaze:
30 ml (2 tbsp) apricot jam

To Decorate:
12 raspberries
4 mint leaves

Peel and core the apples, then slice very thinly, using a mandolin if possible to ensure an even thickness. Immediately sprinkle with lemon juice to prevent browning. Put the apple slices in a heavy-based saucepan with the sugar and lemon juice. Poach lightly, ensuring the apple slices still hold their shape. Turn into a shallow dish and leave to cool completely.

Soak the gelatine leaves in cold water to cover until soft.

To make the crème patissière, whisk the egg yolks and sugar together until pale. Fold in the flour. Heat the milk to just below simmering point, then pour on to the egg mixture, whisking constantly. Strain into a clean pan, stirring until thickened. Add vanilla essence to taste. Cover the surface with dampened greaseproof paper to prevent a skin forming and leave until cold.

Whip the cream until it is thick enough to hold peaks. Squeeze excess water from the gelatine leaves, then warm the gelatine leaves in a bain-marie, or a bowl over a pan of hot water, until dissolved. Stir the gelatine into the crème patissière, working quickly to ensure the gelatine does not form threads. Fold in the whipped cream.

Assemble the 'mille feuille' on a cake board. Arrange a thin layer of apple slices to form the base. Cover with half of the cream mixture. Repeat the layers, then top with a layer of apples. Leave in the refrigerator for about 20 minutes to set.

Meanwhile make the raspberry sauce. Purée the raspberries in a blender or food processor. Add the sugar and water. Warm through and allow to reduce very slightly. Pass through a sieve to remove the pips and leave to cool. Taste for sweetness. The sauce shouldn't be too sweet; if necessary add a squeeze of lemon juice.

Warm the apricot jam with 15 ml (1 tbsp) water then pass through a sieve to make the glaze.

Brush the 'mille feuille' with apricot glaze, then cut into 4 attractive shapes, using an electric knife if available. Place on individual plates and decorate with raspberries and mint leaves. Surround with the raspberry sauce.

REGIONAL HEATS
THE MIDLANDS
GREGORY LEWIS • VERA BLOOR • JANE O'SULLIVAN

JANE O'SULLIVAN'S MENU

STARTER
Chicken Mousse with Mango and Ginger

MAIN COURSE
Tian of Beef Niçoise
Filo Pastry Baskets of Seasonal Vegetables
Aubergine Purée with Pine Nuts
Fondant Potatoes with Sesame Seeds
"LOVE THIS COMBINATION OF VEGETABLES. VERY REFINED" LOYD

DESSERT
Strawberries with Fine Sablé Biscuits and Orange and Lemon Syllabub

J ane lives in the West Midlands and is married to a dentist, whom she met on joining a dental practice after leaving school. She now spends much of her time looking after their three children. Jane loves making cakes for children's parties and weddings. She also enjoys sewing, decorating and working with the Cubs.

CHICKEN MOUSSE WITH MANGO AND GINGER

Mousse:
100 ml (3½ oz) milk
1 chicken breast
salt and freshly ground black pepper
2 egg whites
100 ml (3½ fl oz) whipping cream
20 g (¾ oz) peeled and grated root ginger,
  blanched
2 mangoes

Sauce:
2 egg yolks
200 g (7 oz) butter, melted
juice of ½ lemon
100 ml (3½ fl oz) whipping cream

To Garnish:
few chives

To make the mousse, bring the milk to the boil, then allow to cool. Mince the chicken breast finely in a food processor or using a fine mincer. Season with salt and pepper, then mix in the egg whites. Quickly mix in the cream, cold milk and ginger. Leave to chill in the refrigerator.

Peel and slice the mangoes. Using an aspic cutter, cut out enough shapes from the mango slices to line the bases of 4 ramekins. Reserve the remaining mango slices for garnish. Pour the mousse into the ramekins. Place in a bain marie or roasting tin containing enough hot water to come halfway up the sides of the ramekins. Cook in a preheated oven at 180°C (350°F) mark 4 for about 40 minutes until firm.

For the sauce, whip the egg yolks with 45 ml (3 tbsp) water in a saucepan over gentle heat until slightly thickened. Transfer to a food processor or blender, then, with the machine running, gradually add the melted butter a little at a time. Add salt, pepper and lemon juice. Whip the cream until it just forms soft peaks, then slowly add to the sauce. Whip the sauce until smooth.

To serve, unmould the mousses onto individual serving plates and pour a ribbon of sauce around each one. Garnish with the reserved mango slices and chives.

TIAN OF BEEF NIÇOISE

4 large tomatoes
1 small onion
60 ml (4 tbsp) olive oil
salt and freshly ground black pepper
15 ml (1 tbsp) chopped basil
450 g (1 lb) fresh spinach leaves
freshly grated nutmeg
50 g (2 oz) butter
225 g (8 oz) button mushrooms
300 g (10 oz) beef fillet, in one piece
6 cloves garlic

Sauce:
170 ml (6 fl oz) red wine
300 ml (10 fl oz) beef stock
salt and freshly ground black pepper
50 g (2 oz) butter, diced

To Garnish:
parsley or other fresh herb sprigs

Skin, halve and seed the tomatoes, then chop coarsely. Chop the onion. Heat 30 ml (2 tbsp) of the oil in a saucepan. Add the onion and tomatoes and allow to sweat until the moisture has evaporated and the tomatoes are softened and mashable. Season with salt and pepper and flavour with the chopped basil.

Devein the spinach. Blanch briefly in boiling water, then drain and refresh. Squeeze out as much moisture as possible, then chop. Add a little grated nutmeg to taste and sauté in a little of the butter until just tender. Remove from the heat.

Chop the mushrooms finely and sauté in a little oil until they release their liquid. Remove from the heat.

Cut the fillet of beef down the centre line. Tie each piece of beef with string to hold its shape. Melt the remaining butter in a frying pan, add the garlic and sauté each piece of beef for 4-5 minutes,

turning to brown evenly, until it is cooked but still pink inside. Wrap the beef in foil and keep warm. Reserve the garlic.

To make the sauce, deglaze the pan by adding the red wine and stirring to scrape up the sediment. Simmer to reduce to approximately 10 ml (2 tsp). Add the stock, salt and pepper, and bring to the boil. Reduce by one quarter, then strain into a clean pan; keep warm.

To assemble the tian, reheat each of the vegetables. Rub a little of the fried garlic on the base of each plate and place a metal ring (ie a muffin ring or scone cutter) in the centre of each. Put the spinach in the bottom of the rings, in a fine layer, pressing down with a fork to spread and pack well. Cover with a layer of mushrooms, then place the tomatoes on top. Slice the beef finely and arrange on top of the tomato, to resemble the spokes of a wheel.

Quickly stir the 50 g (2 oz) diced butter into the hot sauce. Spoon a little on the top and around the base of each tian. Carefully remove the ring. Garnish with parsley or other herb sprigs.

Filo Pastry Baskets of Seasonal Vegetables

75 g (3 oz) butter, melted
6 sheets filo pastry
2 carrots
2 courgettes
4 broccoli florets
4 cauliflower florets
10 ml (2 tsp) finely chopped parsley

Use one third of the butter to prepare the filo baskets. Grease 4 patty tins. Lay a sheet of filo on the work surface, brush with melted butter and cover with a second layer of pastry. Brush with melted butter and cover with a third layer. Using a sharp knife, cut out four 12 cm (5 inch) squares (see note). Place each triple layer of squares in a patty tin, pressing the pastry into the base of the tin and allowing the edges to spread out like a handkerchief. Use the pastry trimming to make handles. Place these on a baking tray.

Bake in a preheated oven at 200°C (400°F) mark 6 for 8-10 minutes until the pastry is golden brown. Allow to cool in the tins, then remove and set aside.

To prepare the carrots and courgettes, cut into 4 cm (1½ inch) lengths and shape into batons. Place in a steaming basket with the broccoli and cauliflower. Cook until the vegetables are just tender.

In a bowl, stir together the remaining 50 g (2 oz) butter and chopped parsley. Add the hot vegetables and toss gently to coat in the butter. Place each pastry basket on a small plate and divide the vegetables between them. Add a pastry handle to each basket and serve.

Note: Depending on the size of the filo pastry sheets, you may only be able to cut 3 complete squares. In this case, assemble the fourth from the trimmings.

Aubergine Purée with Pine Nuts

450 g (1 lb) aubergines
40 g (1½ oz) butter, softened
75 g (3 oz) full-fat cream cheese with garlic
1.25 ml (¼ tsp) cayenne pepper
salt
40 g (1½ oz) pine nuts
coriander leaves to garnish

Place the whole unpeeled aubergines under a preheated high grill for approximately 15-20 minutes, turning continuously until they are black all over and the skin has blistered. Holding the hot aubergines in a cloth, break them open and scrape the flesh out into a food processor or blender, using a metal spoon.

Add the butter and soft cheese and work to a smooth purée. Season to taste with cayenne pepper and salt. Spoon the mixture into a warm serving bowl.

Heat a small dry frying pan and add the pine nuts. Toss for 1-2 minutes or until toasted dark brown.

Scatter the nuts over the aubergine purée. Cover the dish with foil and keep warm in a low oven until ready to serve. Garnish with a sprinkling of cayenne pepper and coriander leaves.

Fondant Potatoes with Sesame Seeds

450 g (1 lb) small new potatoes
65 g (2½ oz) unsalted butter
15 ml (1 tbsp) sesame seeds
salt

Scrape the potatoes, rinse in cold water and dry them in a cloth.

Melt two thirds of the butter in a sauté pan. Add the potatoes and shake the pan to coat the potatoes with butter. Cover the pan and cook over a moderate heat for 20-30 minutes, shaking the pan now and then to prevent the potatoes from sticking.

When cooked, remove the lid and increase the heat to drive off any surplus moisture and give the potatoes a crisp finish. Add the remaining butter and, when melted, add the sesame seeds. Shake the pan until the potatoes are evenly coated with sesame seeds. Serve immediately.

STRAWBERRIES WITH FINE SABLÉ BISCUITS AND ORANGE AND LEMON SYLLABUB

Biscuits:

100 g (4 oz) plain flour
40 g (1½ oz) caster sugar
2.5 ml (½ tsp) grated lemon zest
75 g (3 oz) unsalted butter
2 egg yolks

Coulis:

300 g (10 oz) strawberries
15-30 ml (2-3 tbsp) icing sugar
60 ml (2 fl oz) Cointreau

Syllabub:

50 g (2 oz) caster sugar
½ wine glass sherry
juice and finely grated zest of ½ orange
juice and finely grated zest of ½ lemon
300 ml (½ pint) double cream

To Serve:

350 g (12 oz) strawberries
75 g (3 oz) double cream
icing sugar for dusting

To make the biscuits, mix the flour, sugar and lemon zest in a bowl and rub in the butter until the mixture resembles fine breadcrumbs. Add the egg yolks and mix until smooth. Wrap in cling film and leave to rest in the refrigerator for about 20 minutes until the dough is firm enough to roll out.

Roll out the dough thinly and cut out 8 rounds with a fluted 7.5 cm (3 inch) cutter. Cook in a preheated oven at 200°C (400°F) mark 6 for 8 minutes. Transfer to a rack to cool.

To make the coulis, purée the strawberries with some of the icing sugar and the Cointreau in a blender or food processor. Taste for sweetness and add more icing sugar if necessary. Pass through a sieve.

To make the syllabub, mix together the sugar, sherry, orange and lemon zest and juice. Whisk the cream until it forms soft peaks, then add to the sherry mixture. Beat until stiff.

To serve, spread some strawberry coulis on each plate. Very lightly whip the cream and pipe a pattern around the edge of the coulis. Put one biscuit on each plate and place a spoonful of syllabub in the middle. Enclose the syllabub with strawberries, reserving a few with stalks for decoration. Position the remaining biscuits on top of the strawberries and sift over some icing sugar to decorate. Halve the reserved strawberries, glaze with a little coulis and use to decorate the biscuits.

Regional Heats
The East

Tim Souster • Chris Duckham • Joy Skipper

———— Winner ————

Tim Souster's Menu

Starter

Congee of Three Continents

"It is not quite what I expected but the taste is very good" Jane
Asher

"Excellent and fascinating" Loyd

Main Course

*Fish Pie Dauphinoise with an Anchovy and
Tarragon Mustard Sauce
'Nero' Salad*

Dessert

Cassata Norvègienne

Tim lives in Cambridge and is married to a commissioning
editor for Cambridge University Press. They have two
daughters. Tim is a composer who won the BAFTA award for
'Best TV Music for 1990' for 'The Green Man'. He also
wrote the music for the documentary 'Monsoon', a spin off
of which is being performed at the South Bank. He is
presently working on a 'First Tuesday' documentary.
Tim collects 30's pottery and bells.

CONGEE OF THREE CONTINENTS

90 ml (3 fl oz) Thai glutinous rice
600 ml (1 pint) chicken stock
1 Chinese wind-dried sausage
1 Mexican chorizo sausage
125 g (4 oz) piece Italian pepper salami
few drops of sesame oil
chopped garlic chives or spring onions to
*   garnish*

Put the rice in a saucepan with the chicken stock and 1.2 litres (2 pints) water. Simmer for about 45 minutes. Skin and slice the sausages and salami. Add them to the rice and cook for a further 15 minutes.

Divide the rice mixture between individual serving bowls and top each portion with a drop of sesame oil. Garnish with chopped chives or spring onions to serve.

'NERO' SALAD

Select your salad leaves according to whatever looks good on the day!

assorted salad leaves, eg curly endive,
*   fennel, chicory, rocket, radicchio, lollo*
*   rosso*
½ clove garlic
50 g (2 oz) Parmesan cheese, freshly grated
2 anchovy fillets, finely chopped
1 large egg, size 1 or 2
a little olive oil (optional)
lemon juice to taste

Garlic Croûtons:
4 slices baguette
butter, for spreading
1 clove garlic, crushed

First make the garlic croûtons. Butter the baguette slices and spread lightly with crushed garlic. Cut off the crusts and dice the bread. Place on a baking tray and bake in a preheated oven at 180°C (350°F) mark 4 for 15 minutes. Allow to cool.

Tear the salad leaves into manageable pieces. Rub a salad bowl with the cut garlic clove and add the salad leaves. Sprinkle with the cheese and anchovies. Boil the egg for 1 minute only, then break over the salad and toss well. Moisten if necessary with a little olive oil and lemon juice to taste.

Just before serving, sprinkle the garlic croûtons over the salad.

FISH PIE DAUPHINOISE WITH AN ANCHOVY AND MUSTARD SAUCE

Bouquet Garni:
1 leek, white part only
1 tarragon sprig
1 parsley sprig
few chervil sprigs
2 bay leaves
1 blade of mace

Pie Filling:
2 medium salmon steaks
225 g (8 oz) cod, coley, whiting or undyed smoked haddock fillet
600 ml (1 pint) milk
salt and freshly ground black pepper
450 g (1 lb) waxy potatoes, eg Fir-apple, Charlotte or Belle de Fontenay
50 g (2 oz) butter
2 cloves garlic, crushed

Sauce:
1 bay leaf
4 peppercorns
1 slice carrot
1 slice onion
40 g (1½ oz) butter
40 g (1½ oz) flour
4 anchovy fillets, finely chopped
15 ml (1 tbsp) French tarragon mustard
juice of ½ lemon

To Garnish:
coriander sprigs

To assemble the bouquet garni, split the leek in half lengthwise. Place the tarragon, parsley, chervil, bay leaves and mace between the two split leek halves. Secure with string.

Place the fish in an ovenproof dish, pour over the milk and add the bouquet garni, salt and pepper. Cook in a pre-heated oven at 180°C (350°F) mark 4 for 30 minutes until just tender; do not overcook. Meanwhile, parboil the potatoes in boiling salted water for 2-3 minutes only, then drain thoroughly.

Remove the cooked fish from the ovenproof dish, reserving the liquid, then remove any skin and bones. Carefully flake the fish and place in a bowl, toss gently to mix.

Slice the potatoes very thinly, using a mandoline or food processor, leaving the skins on. Grease 4 individual 300 ml (½ pint) oval earthenware pie dishes with butter, then line with baking parchment. Trim the edges, then brush the inside of the paper with oil.

Cover the base and sides of the dishes with a layer of potato slices. Two-thirds fill with the fish filling and cover the top with several layers of potato slices. Dot with the butter and crushed garlic and bake in the oven at 190°C (375°F) mark 5 for 40 minutes.

Meanwhile make the sauce. Strain the reserved milk into a saucepan and add the bay leaf, peppercorns, carrot and onion. Slowly bring to the boil and simmer over a low heat for a few minutes, then strain. Melt the butter in a saucepan, stir in the flour and cook, stirring, for 1 minute. Gradually add the milk, stirring continuously. Cook for 2-3 minutes, then add the anchovies, mustard and lemon juice.

Turn the cooked fish pies out on to individual serving plates and surround with the sauce. Garnish with coriander and serve with 'Nero' salad.

CASSATA NORVÈGIENNE

Vanilla Ice Cream:
4 egg yolks
125 g (4 oz) caster sugar
300 ml (½ pint) milk
2.5 ml (½ tsp) vanilla essence

Flavoured Ice Cream:
300 ml (½ pint) double cream
50 g (2 oz) caster sugar
8 maraschino cherries, chopped
15 ml (1 tbsp) chopped candied orange peel
50 g (2 oz) flaked almonds

To Assemble:
450 g (1 lb) amaretti biscuits
75 g (3 oz) butter
4 egg whites
125 g (4 oz) caster sugar

To Serve:
dash of Amaretto di Saronno liqueur

To make the vanilla ice cream, whisk the egg yolks and sugar together in a bowl. Heat the milk with the vanilla essence to just below boiling point, then pour on to the egg mixture, whisking constantly. Return to the pan and cook over a low heat, stirring constantly, until thickened. Allow to cool. Transfer to an ice-cream maker and churn for 20-30 minutes, then transfer to an oblong freezerproof container, approximately 20 x 9 x 6 cm (8 x 3½ x 2½ inches), and freeze until firm. If you do not have an ice-cream maker, freeze in a suitable container, whisking occasionally to improve the texture.

To make the flavoured ice cream, whisk the cream with the sugar until thick, then fold in the cherries, candied peel and almonds. Chill in the refrigerator for about 30 minutes.

Remove the vanilla ice cream container from the freezer and spoon out a trough along the middle. Fill with the flavoured mixture and level the surface. Cover and freeze for up to 2 days until required.

Crush the amaretti biscuits then mix with the melted butter. Make a biscuit base in each ovenproof serving dish, pressing down firmly. Chill in the refrigerator for 2 hours.

To make the meringue, whisk the egg whites until stiff, then gradually whisk in the sugar. Just before serving, cut 4 thick slices of cassata ice cream and place one on each biscuit base. Spread the meringue over the ice cream to cover completely and immediately bake in the top of a very hot oven at 230°C (450°F) mark 8 for up to 3 minutes to brown the tops. Sprinkle a little liqueur over each dessert and serve immediately.

Regional Heats
The East
TIM SOUSTER • CHRIS DUCKHAM • JOY SKIPPER

CHRIS DUCKHAM'S MENU

STARTER
*Fillet of Turbot on a bed of Leeks with a Shallot
and Oyster Sauce*

MAIN COURSE
*Saddle of Venison with a Juniper and Port Sauce
Parsnip and Apple Cakes
Steamed Asparagus*
"AN EXTRA HELPING OF THIS" LOYD

DESSERT
Strawberry Croustades with a Clementine Sauce
"I WOULD BE VERY HAPPY TO EAT THAT MEAL" JANE ASHER

Chris is a village G.P. working at a health centre and the
Horncastle Cottage Hospital. He lives in Horncastle,
Lincolnshire in a nineteenth century farmhouse, where he has
an interesting and comprehensive wine cellar. Dr Duckham's
practice covers 250 square miles and he and his three
partners share 7500 patients.

FILLET OF TURBOT ON A BED OF LEEKS WITH A SHALLOT AND OYSTER SAUCE

4 turbot fillets, each about 75 g (3 oz)
salt and freshly ground black pepper
25 g (1 oz) unsalted butter

Sauce:
50 g (2 oz) unsalted butter
2 shallots, finely chopped
150 ml (¼ pint) dry white wine
8 shelled oysters with their juice, strained
22.5 ml (1½ tbsp) lemon juice
30 ml (2 tbsp) soured cream
dash of tabasco sauce

Leeks:
25 g (1 oz) unsalted butter
3 medium leeks, diced
30 ml (2 tbsp) dry white wine
30 ml (2 tbsp) double cream

To Garnish:
chervil sprigs

First prepare the sauce. Melt the butter in a pan, add the shallots and sweat them for a few minutes, without browning. Add the white wine and simmer until reduced by half. Add the oysters, their juice and the lemon juice and poach for 2 minutes without boiling. Purée in a blender or food processor until smooth. Add the soured cream and a dash of tabasco. Rub through a sieve, then gently warm the sauce and adjust the seasoning.

To prepare the leeks, melt the butter in a pan, add the leeks and sweat them for 1-2 minutes. Add the white wine and cream and cook for a few minutes more. Season with salt and pepper to taste.

Season the turbot fillets with salt and pepper. Melt the butter in an ovenproof sauté pan and fry the turbot for 15 seconds on each side. Transfer to a preheated oven at 180°C (350°F) mark 4 for 4-5 minutes until cooked. Allow to rest in a warm place for a few minutes.

To serve, place some of the leek mixture on each serving plate. Top with a turbot fillet and pour the sauce around. Garnish with sprigs of chervil.

SADDLE OF VENISON WITH A JUNIPER AND PORT SAUCE

25 g (1 oz) butter
15 ml (1 tbsp) walnut oil
2 fillets of venison, each about 225 g (8 oz),
    taken from the saddle

Sauce:
300 ml (½ pint) game stock
150 ml (¼ pint) port
12 juniper berries, crushed
50 g (2 oz) unsalted butter, in pieces
salt and freshly ground black pepper

First make the sauce. Put the game stock, port and juniper berries in a saucepan and simmer until reduced by half. Off the heat, whisk in the unsalted butter, a piece at a time. Pass through a muslin-lined sieve into a bowl and season with salt and freshly ground black pepper to taste.

In a roasting tin, heat the butter with the walnut oil. Add the venison fillets and quickly sear all over on a high heat. Transfer to a preheated oven at 200°C (400°F) mark 6 and roast for 10 minutes. Cover with foil and leave to rest for a few minutes in a warm place, then carve into fine slices.

To serve, arrange a circle of venison slices on each serving plate and surround with the sauce. Serve with asparagus, and parsnip and apple cakes.

PARSNIP AND APPLE CAKES

2 medium parsnips
2 Golden Delicious apples
25 g (1 oz) butter, melted
45 ml (3 tbsp) chopped chives
2 egg yolks
45 ml (3 tbsp) plain flour
butter, for frying

Peel halve and core the parsnips and apples, then grate finely and place in a bowl. Add the melted butter, chives, egg yolks and flour; mix thoroughly until evenly incorporated.

Form the mixture into small 'cakes'. Heat about 50 g (2 oz) butter in a frying pan and fry the parsnip and apple cakes for 2-3 minutes on each side. Drain on absorbent kitchen paper and serve.

Note: These can be prepared ahead and reheated in a hot oven when required.

STRAWBERRY CROUSTADES WITH A CLEMENTINE SAUCE

Pastry Croustades:
200 g (7 oz) plain flour, sifted
70 g (2¾ oz) caster sugar
1 small egg, size 6 or 7
100 g (3½ oz) butter, softened

Clementine Sauce:
8 clementines
3.75 ml (¾ tsp) arrowroot
20 g (¾ oz) caster sugar

Strawberry Mousse:
225 g (8 oz) strawberries
300 ml (10 fl oz) double cream
32 g (1¼ oz) caster sugar
10 ml (2 tsp) fraises des bois (wild
  strawberry) liqueur

To Decorate:
mint leaves

For the pastry croustades, mix the flour with the sugar, egg and butter to make a smooth dough. Roll out thinly on a lightly floured surface and use to line 4 oiled small savarin moulds. Prick the dough all over with a fork and bake in a preheated oven at 180°C (350°F) mark 4 for 10 minutes. Ease the croustades out of their moulds while still warm and transfer to a wire rack to cool.

To make the clementine sauce, halve the clementines and squeeze to extract their juice. Mix the arrowroot with a little of the clementine juice. Dissolve the sugar in the remaining juice in a saucepan over a moderate heat. Increase the heat and bring to the boil. Add the blended arrowroot to the boiling mixture and cook, stirring, until thickened. Strain and leave to cool.

For the strawberry mousse, set aside 4 strawberries for decoration, then hull the remainder and purée in a blender or food processor until smooth. Pass through a sieve to remove the pips. Whip the double cream with the caster sugar until soft peaks form. Fold the strawberry purée into the whipped cream, with the liqueur.

To serve, fill each pastry croustade with strawberry mousse and invert onto a serving plate. Place a little of the mousse mixture on the middle of each one and pour the clementine sauce around the croustades. Decorate with the reserved strawberries and mint.

REGIONAL HEATS
THE EAST

TIM SOUSTER • CHRIS DUCKHAM • JOY SKIPPER

JOY SKIPPER'S MENU

STARTER
Mussel and Almond Soup
"SOUPS THAT THICK ARE QUITE COMFORTING TO EAT.
A VERY INTERESTING IDEA" SHAUN HILL

MAIN COURSE
*Salmon, Leek and Ginger Nests served with a Leek and
Tomato Sauce
Timbale of Courgettes
Mangetout*

DESSERT
Raspberry Pavlovas with a Raspberry and Sloe Gin Coulis
"LOVELY SAUCE. VERY, VERY GOOD" JANE ASHER

Joy lives in Wymondham, Norfolk. After working for Anglia TV and as a window dresser, she decided to return to college to study photography. She has just completed her course at the Norwich College of Arts and Technology, specialising in food photography, and starts work in a London studio later this year. Joy's other great passion is horses, and she has helped train many a show winner.

MUSSEL AND ALMOND SOUP

450 g (1 lb) mussels
100 g (4 oz) butter
2 carrots, sliced
2 onions, sliced
2 parsnips, sliced
225 g (8 oz) button mushrooms
10 ml (2 tsp) flour
600 ml (1 pint) water
parsley sprig
12 blanched almonds
4 hard-boiled egg yolks
150 ml (¼ pint) single cream
salt and freshly ground pepper

Scrub the mussels thoroughly, removing their beards, and discard any open or cracked ones.

Melt 50 g (2 oz) butter in a saucepan, add the vegetables and cook, stirring occasionally, until slightly browned. Sprinkle in the flour and cook, stirring, for 3 minutes. Gradually stir in the water, cover and cook for 40 minutes.

Melt the remaining 50 g (2 oz) butter in another pan. Add the mussels with the parsley, cover and cook until the shells open; discarding any that remain closed. Set aside 8 mussels in their shells, then shell the rest of them. Reserve the cooking liquid.

When the vegetables are cooked, remove them with a slotted spoon and place in a blender or food processor, with the shelled mussels, almonds and egg yolks. Work until smooth, then return to the soup. Strain the mussel cooking liquid and add to the pan. Add the cream, adjust the seasoning and serve the soup garnished with the mussels in shells.

TIMBALE OF COURGETTES

75 g (3 oz) butter
450 g (1 lb) courgettes
salt and freshly ground black pepper
1 small onion, chopped
50 g (2 oz) Gruyère cheese, grated
1 egg, beaten
pinch of freshly grated nutmeg

Melt 25 g (1 oz) butter and use to grease 4 ramekins. Cut the courgettes into fine slices, using a potato peeler, and use some of the courgette slices to line the ramekins.

Cook the remaining courgettes briefly in salted water until just tender. Drain well then purée in a blender or food processor until smooth.

Melt the remaining 50 g (2 oz) butter in a small pan and fry the onion until soft. Transfer to a bowl and mix in the cheese, egg, nutmeg and salt and pepper. Add the courgette purée and mix thoroughly.

Divide the mixture between the ramekins. Place them in a roasting tin containing enough water to come halfway up the sides of the ramekins. Bake in a preheated oven at 170°C (325°F) mark 3 for about 25-30 minutes.

Let cool for 5 minutes, then loosen the edge of each timbale with a blunt-edged knife. Carefully turn out each one on to a serving plate.

Salmon, Leek and Ginger Nests with a Leek and Tomato Sauce

2 fillets of salmon, each about 175 g (6 oz)
50 g (2 oz) butter
4 sheets filo pastry
2 leeks
dill sprig

Marinade:

30 ml (2 tbsp) honey
30 ml (2 tbsp) olive oil
30 ml (2 tbsp) soy sauce
2.5 cm (1 inch) piece fresh root ginger,
   peeled and roughly chopped

Sauce:

50 ml (3½ tbsp) white wine
1 leek, sliced
50 ml (3½ tbsp) double cream
250 g (9 oz) unsalted butter
50 g (2 oz) tomato concassé
salt and freshly ground pepper

Remove the skin from the salmon, tweeze out any tiny bones, then cut into bite-sized pieces. Mix together the ingredients for the marinade in a shallow dish. Add the salmon, cover and leave to marinate in the refrigerator for 1 hour.

Melt half of the butter. Brush the sheets of filo pastry with melted butter, fold each one in half and use to line 7.5 cm (3 inch) individual flan tins, trimming away excess pastry. Brush with butter and bake blind in a preheated oven at 200°C (400°F) mark 6 for 5 minutes or until golden.

Slice the leeks crosswise very thinly. Melt the remaining 25 g (1 oz) butter in a frying pan and fry the leeks until softened. Transfer to the filo pastry nests, using a slotted spoon.

Very quickly fry the salmon in the fat remaining in the pan to seal, then place on top of the leeks, allowing 3 or 4 pieces for each nest. Return to the oven for 5 minutes.

To make the sauce, bring the wine to the boil in a saucepan, add the leek and boil until reduced by half. Add the cream, then add the butter, a little at a time, over a moderate heat, shaking the pan until all of the butter has melted. Add the tomato concassé and seasoning to taste.

Serve the salmon nests, garnished with dill and accompanied by the leek and tomato sauce, and timbale of courgettes.

Note: For the tomato concassé, simply peel and seed a few tomatoes, then finely chop the flesh.

RASPBERRY PAVLOVAS WITH A RASPBERRY AND SLOE GIN COULIS

Pavlovas:
2 egg whites
100 g (4 oz) caster sugar

Coulis:
100 g (4 oz) sugar
finely pared rind of 1 orange
1 cinnamon stick
150 ml (¼ pint) water
150 ml (¼ pint) sloe gin
225 g (8 oz) raspberries

Syrup:
finely pared rind of 2 oranges
8 green peppercorns in brine, drained
100 g (4 oz) sugar
150 ml (¼ pint) water

To Serve:
150 ml (¼ pint) double cream, whipped
225 g (8 oz) raspberries

To make the pavlovas, whisk the egg whites until stiff, then gradually beat in the sugar, 25 g (1 oz) at a time. Spoon the meringue mixture into 8 even-sized mounds on a baking sheet lined with oiled greaseproof paper. Place in a preheated oven at 150°C (300°F) mark 2. Immediately lower the temperature to 140°C (275°F) mark 1 and bake for 1 hour, then turn off the oven, leaving the pavlovas to cool in the oven.

To make the coulis, put the sugar, orange rind and cinnamon in a saucepan with water and heat gently until the sugar has dissolved. Increase the heat, add the sloe gin and boil rapidly to reduce. Add the raspberries and leave to cool.

Discard the orange rind. Purée in a blender or food processor, then pass through a sieve to remove the pips.

To make the green peppercorn and orange syrup, cut the orange rind into strips and place in a saucepan with the peppercorns, sugar and water. Slowly bring to the boil, then simmer until reduced to a syrupy consistency.

Spread a pool of raspberry coulis on each serving plate and place a meringue on the coulis. Cover the meringue with whipped cream and raspberries. Pour over some of the orange syrup. Place a second meringue on top of the raspberries, setting it at an angle. Decorate the coulis with a splash of cream, feathered with a skewer. Serve immediately.

REGIONAL HEATS

THE HOME COUNTIES

NANCY SMITH • MARK JAMES • KEITH KEER

WINNER

NANCY SMITH'S MENU

STARTER

Salmon Mille Feuille with a Shallot Sauce

"VERY INTENSE SAUCE" RUTH ROGERS

"MUCH MORE COMPLEX TASTING THAN I THOUGHT IT WOULD BE" LOYD

MAIN COURSE

Roast Saddle of Lamb with a Leek Sauce

Boulangère Potatoes

Quenelles of Carrot and Swede

DESSERT

LEMON MOUSSE WITH HONEY WAFERS

Living in Middlesex, Nancy began work as a dental nurse, then joined the accounts department of the Foreign Office. At 21 she went back to college to read Geography as a mature student. She now works at the Stock Exchange. Nancy's leisure pursuits include cycling, swimming, hiking, playing tennis and badminton.

SALMON MILLE FEUILLE WITH A SHALLOT SAUCE

Puff Pastry:
350 g (12 oz) plain flour
pinch of salt
175 g (6 oz) margarine
175 g (6 oz) lard
12 ml (¾ tbsp) lemon juice
about 170 ml (6 fl oz) chilled water

Salmon Filling:
5 ml (1 tsp) butter
450 g (1 lb) salmon fillet, very thinly sliced

Sauce:
15 g (½ oz) butter
1 shallot, finely chopped
125 ml (4 fl oz) dry white wine
250 ml (8 fl oz) cream
salt and cayenne pepper

To Garnish:
chervil sprigs

To make the puff pastry, sift the flour and salt together into a bowl. Add the margarine and lard in walnut-sized lumps and mix into the flour. Make a well in the centre and add the lemon juice and sufficient water to mix to a soft, elastic dough.

On a floured surface, roll out the pastry to a rectangle. Fold into three, seal the edges with a rolling pin and roll out again to a rectangle. Repeat 4 times. Wrap in greaseproof paper and chill in the refrigerator for 1 hour.

Roll the pastry out thinly to a large rectangle, measuring about 38 x 30 cm (15 x 12 inches), and prick the surface with a fork. Place on a baking sheet and place a wire rack over the pastry to prevent it rising during cooking. Bake in a preheated oven at 220°C (425°F) mark 7 for 15 minutes, then lower the temperature to 180°C (350°F) mark 4 and bake for a further 15 minutes.

To prepare the sauce, melt the butter in a saucepan, add the shallot and cook until softened. Add the wine and allow to reduce until the liquid evaporates. Add the cream and season with salt and cayenne pepper to taste; keep warm.

To make the salmon filling, melt the butter in a pan, add the salmon and cook over medium heat for 2 seconds each side. When the pastry is cooked, cut it into 4 large rectangles. Layer the pastry with the salmon mixture, finishing with a layer of puff pastry.

Cut the salmon mille feuille into four equal portions and place on individual serving plates. Pour the shallot sauce over the top and garnish with chervil leaves to serve.

ROAST SADDLE OF LAMB WITH A LEEK SAUCE

15 g (½ oz) butter
30 ml (2 tbsp) oil
2 short saddles of lamb
6 thyme sprigs
3 coriander sprigs
salt and freshly ground black pepper
1 large clove garlic

Sauce:
700 g (½ lb) leeks
25 g (1 oz) butter
1 clove garlic, crushed
75 ml (5 tbsp) double cream
10 ml (2 tbsp) lemon juice
a little milk to mix

First prepare the sauce. Trim the leeks, reserving the green tops for garnish. Chop the leeks. Melt the butter in a saucepan, add the leeks and cook over a low heat until softened. Add the garlic and sweat until softened. Purée the leek mixture in a blender or food processor, then pass through a sieve. Put the double cream in a saucepan and slowly bring to the boil to thin out, then add the lemon juice and leeks. Season with salt and pepper and add just enough milk to give a pouring consistency. Keep warm on one side, until ready to serve.

Heat the butter and oil in a roasting tin in a preheated oven at 220°C (425°F) mark 7. Rub the meat with the herbs and seasoning. Cut the garlic into slivers and insert into the meat at regular intervals. Place the meat in the hot fat and turn to seal on both sides. Put the herb sprigs on top of the meat and cook in the oven for 5 minutes on each side. Meanwhile blanch the reserved leek tops in boiling salted water; drain thoroughly and cut into diamonds.

When cooked, slice the lamb and arrange the slices fanned out on warmed serving plates. Pour the sauce over the meat and garnish with the leek diamonds. Serve immediately, with the vegetable accompaniments.

BOULANGÈRE POTATOES

1 kg (2 lb) Red Desirée or Cara potatoes
salt and freshly ground black pepper
1 large onion, finely chopped
150 ml (¼ pint) vegetable stock
150 ml (¼ pint) milk
50 g (2 oz) butter, in pieces

Peel the potatoes and cut into medium slices. Parboil in boiling salted water for 1 minute. Layer the potato slices in a buttered baking dish with the onion and seasoning. Pour over the vegetable stock and milk; dot with the butter. Cover the dish with foil and cook on the top shelf of a preheated oven at 180°C (350°F) mark 4 for 30 minutes, removing the foil for the last 15 minutes to brown and crisp the top.

QUENELLES OF CARROT AND SWEDE

4 medium carrots
½ small swede
salt and freshly ground black pepper
large knob of butter

Cut the carrots and swede into even-sized pieces and cook separately in boiling salted water until tender. Drain thoroughly, then combine the vegetables and mash with butter until smooth. Season with salt and pepper to taste.

Using two dessertspoons, shape the vegetable purée into quenelles on serving plates. Serve immediately.

LEMON MOUSSE

22 g (¾ oz) powdered gelatine
125 ml (4 fl oz) hot water
finely grated rind and juice of 2 lemons
300 ml (½ pint) double cream
50 g (2 oz) caster sugar
2 egg whites

To Decorate:
mint sprigs
jellied lemon segments

Sprinkle the gelatine on to the hot water, stir until dissolved, then allow to cool. Add the lemon rind and juice.

Whip the cream until thick, then whisk in the sugar. Whisk the egg whites until stiff. When the lemon mixture is cool, fold into the whipped cream mixture. Fold in the whisked egg whites, then divide between ramekins. Chill in the refrigerator for about 5 hours or overnight until firm.

When the mousses are set, dip the base of each ramekin in a bowl of boiling water for 1 second, then turn out each mousse on to a serving plate. Decorate each one with a sprig of mint and a jellied lemon segment.

HONEY WAFERS

15 g (½ oz) butter, melted
20 g (¾ oz) icing sugar, sifted
15 ml (1 tbsp) clear honey
20 g (¾ oz) plain flour
pinch of ground ginger
½ egg white

Grease a large baking sheet and place in the freezer to chill thoroughly.

In a bowl, mix together the melted butter and icing sugar, then add the honey. Stir in the flour and ginger, then finally mix in the egg white to give a smooth paste consistency. Cover and chill in the refrigerator for 30 minutes.

Spoon the chilled mixture into 7.5 cm (3 inch) rounds on the chilled baking sheet, spacing well apart to allow for spreading. Bake in a preheated oven at 220°C (425°F) mark 7 for 3 minutes until golden.

While still soft, lift each wafer using a palette knife and drape over a rolling pin. Leave until firm. Serve with the lemon mousse.

REGIONAL HEATS
THE HOME COUNTIES
NANCY SMITH • MARK JAMES • KEITH KEER

MARK JAMES' MENU

STARTER
Pan-fried Duck Breast on a Salad of Braised Red Cabbage

MAIN COURSE
Scallops on a Celeriac and Potato Pancake with Chervil Beurre Blanc
Winter Vegetables

DESSERT
Baked Pear with Zabaglione and Spiced Wine Sauce served with Caraway and Almond Biscuits
"JUST RIGHT" LOYD

M ark lives in Berkshire in a church lodge and works as an accountant at the Battle Hospital in Reading. In his spare time he runs an AIDS support group in Slough. His interests include music, opera, aromatherapy and acupuncture.

PAN-FRIED DUCK BREAST ON A SALAD OF BRAISED RED CABBAGE

For this starter you will need to prepare the braised red cabbage the day before serving.

2.5 ml (½ tsp) salt
2 large duck breasts, each
   weighing 275 g (10 oz)
4 handfuls of mixed salad leaves,
   eg radicchio, curly endive, lamb's
   lettuce, sorrel
Braised Red Cabbage (see right)

Orange Dressing:
1 orange
5 ml (1 tsp) white wine vinegar
5 ml (1 tsp) Dijon mustard
salt and freshly ground black pepper
15-25 ml (3-5 tsp) olive oil

To Serve:
15 ml (1 tbsp) raisins
15 ml (1 tbsp) toasted pine nuts
1 orange, sliced

Sprinkle the salt into a heavy frying pan and heat. When hot, add the duck breasts, skin side down and sauté for 10 minutes; they will yield a lot of fat. Turn the breasts over and cook the meat side for 4 minutes until tender, but still pink inside. Remove from the pan. Leave in a warm place to rest for 10 minutes.

Meanwhile prepare the orange salad dressing. Finely pare the rind from half of the orange, cut into fine strips and reserve for the garnish. Squeeze the juice from the orange and mix with the vinegar, mustard and seasoning. Whisk in the olive oil to yield a thick emulsion.

Arrange the salad leaves on one half of each serving plate. Place 2 or 3 heaped spoonfuls of the cooled braised cabbage on top of the salad leaves.

Slice the duck breasts into thin diagonal slices and arrange in a fan shape on the other side of each plate. Spoon the orange dressing over the duck and salad. Top with raisins, pine nuts and the reserved orange rind. Garnish with orange slices to serve.

BRAISED RED CABBAGE

30 ml (2 tbsp) olive oil
1 large onion, chopped
1 small red cabbage, cored and finely sliced
1 large cooking apple
15 ml (1 tbsp) brown sugar
60 ml (4 tbsp) red wine vinegar
   (approximately)
2.5 ml (½ tsp) caraway seeds
1 bay leaf
4 allspice berries, crushed
salt and freshly ground black pepper

Heat the oil in a large pan and sauté the onion until soft, but not coloured. Add the red cabbage and cook, stirring, for 10 minutes.

Peel, core and chop the apple and add to the cabbage with the sugar. Cook for a further 5 minutes. Add the remaining ingredients and bring to a gentle simmer. Cover the pan and simmer very gently for 2 hours, adding a little more wine vinegar if the mixture becomes dry.

Leave overnight at room temperature before serving cold.

SCALLOPS ON A CELERIAC AND POTATO PANCAKE

I use a cast-iron griddle to cook these pancakes and scallops. If you haven't got one, use a heavy-based frying pan.

12-16 scallops (depending on size), shelled and cleaned

Pancakes:
2 medium potatoes
175 g (6 oz) celeriac
salt and freshly ground black pepper
oil for frying

Chervil Beurre Blanc:
1 shallot, finely chopped
60 ml (4 tbsp) white wine vinegar
225 g (8 oz) chilled butter, in small cubes
15 ml (1 tbsp) double cream (optional)

First make the pancakes. Coarsely grate the potatoes and celeriac. Place in a clean cloth and squeeze out as much moisture as possible. Turn into a bowl and season with salt and pepper. Toss well.

In a heavy-based frying pan, heat a little oil until it is really hot. Place a 7.5 cm (3 inch) plain metal ring in the pan and put a heaped spoonful of the potato and celeriac mixture in the ring. Push the mixture down with the back of a spoon; the ring gives the 'pancake' a good shape. Remove the ring and flatten the pancake with a spatula. Cook for about 3 minutes until brown and crisp underneath. Turn over and cook the other side, for about 3 minutes. Transfer to a wire rack. Repeat to make 4 pancakes.

To make the chervil beurre blanc, put the shallot, vinegar and seasoning in a heavy-based saucepan and boil until reduced to about 1 tablespoon. Transfer to a bowl and place in a bain marie or over a pan of gently simmering water. Add the chilled butter to the sauce, one piece at a time whisking until thoroughly incorporated before adding the next piece. When all the butter has been added, a foamy sauce will result which must be served as soon as possible. If it begins to separate add the cream and whisk vigorously.

Brush the cleaned pan with oil and heat until hot, then cook the scallops for about 1 minute on each side. Serve immediately, on the pancakes with the chervil beurre blanc.

BAKED PEAR WITH ZABAGLIONE AND SPICED WINE SAUCE

4 ripe pears
60 ml (4 tbsp) perry

Sauce:
1 orange
1 lemon
150 ml (¼ pint) red wine
15 ml (1 tbsp) sugar, or to taste
1 cinnamon stick
2 cloves
freshly grated nutmeg
5 ml (1 tsp) arrowroot

Zabaglione:
4 egg yolks
50 g (2 oz) caster sugar
60 ml (4 tbsp) perry

First make the spiced wine sauce. Finely pare the rind from the orange and lemon, then cut into thin strips; squeeze the juice from both fruit. Put the red wine and the orange and lemon juice in a saucepan with some of the citrus rind strips. Add the sugar and spices and bring to a very gentle simmer. Remove from the heat and allow to steep for 20 minutes. Mix the arrowroot with a little cold water and stir into the wine mixture. Bring to the boil, stirring, until thickened. Strain and allow to cool.

Carefully remove the core from each of the pears, working from the base with an apple corer and a small teaspoon, keeping the pears intact. Place the pears in a casserole dish with the perry and cover the dish with foil. Cook in a preheated oven at 180°C (350°F) mark 4 until the pears are soft, about 20 minutes, depending on ripeness.

To make the zabaglione, whisk the egg yolks and sugar together in a large bowl until pale and increased in volume. Place the bowl in a double boiler or over a pan of simmering water and slowly add the perry, whisking constantly. Continue whisking until the zabaglione is very thick, but avoid overheating. Place the bowl over a container of cold water and whisk until cool.

Put 5 ml (1 tsp) of the spiced wine sauce on the base of each serving plate and place the pear on top. Place a quarter of the zabaglione on the side of each place and serve immediately, with almond and caraway biscuits.

Note: Perry is made in a similar way to cider, but from pears. It is a speciality of Normandy, Brittany and South-west England.

ALMOND AND CARAWAY BISCUITS

100 g (4 oz) plain flour
pinch of salt
50 g (2 oz) caster sugar
50 g (2 oz) butter
about ½ egg, beaten
50 g (2 oz) blanched almonds
2.5 ml (½ tsp) caraway seeds

Put the flour, salt and sugar in a large bowl and rub in the butter until the mixture resembles fine breadcrumbs. Add sufficient egg to bind to a stiff paste. Mix in the whole almonds and caraway seeds.

Form the mixture into a thick sausage shape, wrap in foil and chill in the refrigerator for 30 minutes.

Unwrap the dough, and using a sharp knife, cut into 5 mm (¼ inch) thick slices on the slant; this will produce oval biscuits.

Place the ovals on a greased baking sheet and bake in a preheated oven at 170°C (325°F) mark 3 for 25-30 minutes or until golden brown and crisp. Cool on a wire rack.

REGIONAL HEATS
The Home Counties
Nancy Smith • Mark James • Keith Keer

Keith Keer's Menu

Starter

Chicken, Prawn and Fruit Salad

Main Course

Sea Bass Fillets with Fennel
Crisp Slices of Fennel in a Cream Sauce
Steamed Carrots
Steamed Mangetout

Dessert

Individual Apple Tarts with Calvados flavoured Crème
Chantilly
"Terrific" Loyd

Keith lives in Berkshire, is married and has two children. The general manager of a Volvo garage in Leatherhead, he has been in the motor trade since he left school. Keith's wife is involved in an amateur dramatic group – and Keith likes to do a bit of acting too. He runs, cycles and lifts weights in order to keep up his fitness for waterskiing and playing squash. He enjoys giving dinner parties.

CHICKEN, PRAWN AND FRUIT SALAD

4 cloves garlic, cut into slivers
oil for frying
4 shallots, thinly sliced
225 g (8 oz) skinless chicken breast fillets
16 large raw prawns in shells
60 ml (4 tbsp) roasted peanuts
5 ml (1 tsp) salt
5 ml (1 tsp) sugar
45 ml (3 tbsp) lime juice
3 green chillies
1 large Granny Smith apple
45 ml (3 tbsp) lemon juice
1 orange
selection of salad leaves, eg feuille de chêne
  lamb's lettuce, radicchio
75 g (3 oz) seedless black grapes
75 g (3 oz) seedless green grapes

To Garnish:

few herbs sprigs, eg chervil, salad burnet
few cooked whole prawns (optional)

Fry the garlic slivers in a little oil until crisp, then remove with a slotted spoon and drain on absorbent kitchen paper. Fry the shallots in the oil remaining in the pan until crisp. Drain on absorbent kitchen paper.

Slice the chicken breasts lengthwise and lightly poach in simmering water for 5 minutes. Peel and devein the prawns then poach for 2-3 minutes. Combine the chicken and prawns in a bowl, cover and set aside.

Crush the peanuts lightly and mix with the salt, sugar and lime juice in a small bowl. Cut the chillies into very fine rings.

Peel, core and dice the apple and keep in a bowl of chilled water, with the lemon juice added to prevent discolouration, until required. Peel and segment the orange, discarding all pith. Immediately before serving, drain the apples and dry them.

Coarsely shred some of the salad leaves and arrange in the centre of individual serving plates to form small mounds. Surround with salad leaves and pile the remaining salad ingredients over the mounds. Garnish with herbs and whole prawns, if desired.

Sea Bass Fillets with Fennel

The sea bass fillets should be scaled and have the fins and gills removed.

4 sea bass fillets, each about 175 g (6 oz)
walnut oil for brushing

Trim the sea bass fillets, leaving the skin on. Carefully tweeze away any remaining bones. Score the skin in a diamond pattern, using a sharp knife.

Brush the fish with walnut oil and place on the grill rack. Cook under a preheated very hot grill for 8-10 minutes, turning once. Serve with the fennel in cream sauce, steamed carrots and mangetout.

Crisp Slices of Fennel in a Cream Sauce

2 medium fennel bulbs
15 ml (1 tbsp) olive oil
2 shallots
1 thyme sprig
3 basil leaves
250 ml (8 fl oz) fish stock
15 ml (1 tbsp) Pernod
200 ml (7 fl oz) double cream
50 g (2 oz) chilled butter, diced
salt and freshly ground black pepper
oil for deep-frying

Trim the fennel, reserving the feathery tops. Remove the hard outer layer and reserve, then cut each bulb in half lengthwise. Remove the core, then thinly slice the fennel.

To make the sauce, heat the olive oil in a saucepan, add the shallots and herbs and cook for 5 minutes until golden. Add the fish stock, reserved outer fennel layers and Pernod. Boil steadily for about 10 minutes until reduced to a syrupy consistency. Add the cream and boil to reduce to a sauce consistency. Pass through a sieve, then whisk in the butter, a piece at a time. Season with salt and pepper and add the chopped fennel tops. Keep warm, while frying the fennel.

Heat the oil in a deep-fat fryer until very hot, then deep-fry the fennel slices for about 30 seconds. Drain on absorbent kitchen paper and serve immediately, with the sauce.

Note: Care must be taken to avoid any separation of the sauce.

INDIVIDUAL APPLE TARTS WITH CALVADOS FLAVOURED CRÈME CHANTILLY

For the crème chantilly, it's important to have everything well chilled, so put the bowl and whisk into the refrigerator to chill well beforehand.

1 kg (2¼ lb) Cox's apples
15 g (½ oz) butter
1.25 ml (¼ tsp) ground cinnamon
50 g (2 oz) sugar
120 ml (4 fl oz) Calvados
225 g (8 oz) readymade puff pastry
60 ml (4 tbsp) apricot jam

Crème Chantilly:
120 ml (4 fl oz) chilled whipping cream
25 g (1 oz) icing sugar

Set aside 4 apples. Peel, core and roughly chop the remaining apples. Place in a saucepan over a low heat with the butter. Add the cinnamon, sugar and all but 30 ml (2 tbsp) of the Calvados. Cook until the apples are soft and the mixture is reduced to a sauce, stirring occasionally. Sieve if necessary.

Roll out the pastry as thinly as possible on a lightly floured surface. Using a saucer as a guide, cut out 4 rounds, 1 cm (½ inch) larger than the saucer all round. Bend the edge of the pastry upwards to form a rim around each circle.

Spread the apple sauce over the base of the tarts. Peel, core and thinly slice the reserved apples. Arrange the apple slices over the sauce, making sure it is totally covered. Bake in a preheated oven at 230°C (450°F) mark 8 for 15 minutes. Lower the temperature to 200°C (400°F) mark 6 and bake for a further 10 minutes or until the pastry is golden brown and the apples are caramelised; make sure they do not burn.

Warm the apricot jam with 15 ml (1 tbsp) Calvaldos, then sieve and brush over the apple slices to glaze.

Prepare the crème chantilly a few minutes before serving. Whisk the cream with the icing sugar, adding the reserved 15 ml (1 tbsp) Calvados a little at a time during whisking. Take care to avoid overbeating.

Serve the apple tarts warm, with the crème chantilly.

REGIONAL HEATS
THE SOUTH WEST

ORLANDO MURRIN • JAN GILBERTHORPE • HELEN POTHECARY

WINNER

ORLANDO MURRIN'S MENU

STARTER

Red Pepper Pots with Toasted Cheese Cornbread

"DELICIOUS CORNBREAD. NICE DISH AS A FIRST COURSE" LOYD

MAIN COURSE

Chicken with Roast Garlic in Sauternes Sauce

Fresh Tarragon Noodles

Butter-cooked Lettuce

"I WOULD BE VERY HAPPY JUST TO HAVE THAT AND WISH IT WERE WAITING FOR ME AT HOME" JEAN MARSH

DESSERT

Fig Tart with Scented Cream

"DELICIOUS TO SMELL. YOU COULD PUT IT BEHIND YOUR EARS AS WELL!" LOYD

Orlando lives in London and Wiltshire and has two exotic cats. He read English at Cambridge, and is a classically trained pianist. Orlando is deputy editor of 'Living' magazine, and also writes gardening features. This often involves interviewing celebrities with exceptional gardens. He has just written a Christmas Wine booklet. In his leisure time Orlando loves to entertain, enjoys listening to and playing music, kite flying, tapestry and gardening.

RED PEPPER POTS

This light, fresh purée has a vibrant taste and a ravishing colour.

5 ml (1 tsp) butter
4 red peppers, cored, seeded and roughly
*   chopped*
1 clove garlic, finely sliced
pinch of thyme leaves
15 ml (1 tbsp) wine vinegar
scant 150 ml (¼ pint) double cream
salt and freshly ground black pepper

Melt the butter in a saucepan and add the peppers, garlic and thyme. Cover and cook gently for 25 minutes. Add the vinegar, increase the heat and cook until all excess moisture has evaporated. Purée the mixture in a food processor or blender, then pass through a sieve.

Whip the cream until stiff, then fold in the red pepper purée. Season with salt and pepper to taste. Divide between individual ramekins and serve with toasted cheese cornbread.

CHEESE CORNBREAD

This tasty cornbread is even more delicious toasted.

175 g (6 oz) cornmeal (polenta)
100 g (4 oz) plain flour
15 ml (1 tbsp) caster sugar
10 ml (2 tsp) baking powder
pinch of salt
50 g (2 oz) butter, melted
1 egg, beaten
150 ml (5 fl oz) natural yogurt
200 ml (7 fl oz) milk
50 g (2 oz) Parmesan cheese, freshly grated
15 ml (1 tbsp) finely snipped chives
30 ml (2 tbsp) chopped parsley

Stir together the dry ingredients in a mixing bowl, then make a well in the centre. Mix the melted butter with the egg, yogurt and milk. Pour into the dry ingredients and mix together gently, adding the cheese and herbs, to yield a thick batter.

Turn into a greased and base-lined 20 cm (8 inch) round or 18 cm (7 inch) square tin and bake in a preheated oven at 200°C (400°F) mark 6 for about 30 minutes, until risen and lightly golden. Cool on a wire rack. Serve sliced and toasted if preferred.

CHICKEN WITH ROAST GARLIC IN SAUTERNES SAUCE

This is an exceptional and extravagant main course! Most of the work is in the preparation of the Sauternes sauce base, which can be made in advance if preferred – and in double quantities so that you can freeze half for another occasion. The grilled chicken is tenderised by the crème fraîche, and the garlic is sweet and tender – not at all powerful or pungent.

1 boned chicken, cut into 4 pieces
  (use carcass for sauce)
120 ml (4 fl oz) crème fraîche
4 baby carrots, scrubbed

Sauternes Sauce Base:
30 ml (2 tbsp) olive oil
450 g (1 lb) onions, sliced
450 g (1 lb) carrots, sliced
1 leek, sliced
1 chicken carcass, in pieces
1 kg (2 lb) veal bones
1 bottle Sauternes
450 ml (¾ pint) light chicken stock
bouquet garni, ie parsley sprigs, 2 thyme
  sprigs, celery and bay leaves
75 ml (5 tbsp) double cream
salt and freshly ground black pepper
10 ml (2 tbsp) lemon juice, or to taste

Roast Garlic:
2 heads garlic, unpeeled
15 g (½ oz) butter
10 ml (2 tsp) sugar

To Finish:
15 ml (1 tbsp) chopped parsley

Place the chicken in a dish, pour over the crème fraîche and season with salt and pepper to taste. Leave to marinate in a cool place while preparing the sauce.

To make the Sauternes sauce base, heat the oil in a large pan and add the onions, carrots and leek. Cover and cook for 5 minutes, then uncover and cook for about 15 minutes until browned. Add the chicken carcass and veal bones. Cook for about 10 minutes until browned.

Add a cupful of Sauternes and cook for about 20 minutes until reduced to a glaze. Repeat until all the Sauternes is used. Lower the heat and add the stock and bouquet garni. Cover and cook for 1 hour. Strain through a fine sieve, pressing to extract as much juice as possible. Cook until reduced to a cupful, about 10 minutes. Allow to cool, then remove any fat from the surface.

To prepare the garlic, add to a small pan of boiling water and boil for 3 minutes, then drain and remove the skins. Heat the butter in an ovenproof dish, add the garlic and sprinkle with the sugar. Cook in a preheated oven at 120°C (250°F) mark ½ (or at the bottom of a hotter oven while other dishes cook) for about 2 hours. The garlic should be tender and golden; if necessary cover with foil during cooking to prevent browning.

Cook the chicken under a preheated grill for 5-10 minutes, then turn over and grill for 5-10 minutes until tender and cooked through. Remove the chicken as it is cooked; the legs will take longer.

Meanwhile cook the carrots in boiling salted water for 1 minute; drain.

Bring the sauce to the boil, then add the cream and reduce slightly. Correct the seasoning and add lemon juice if necessary. Slice the chicken attractively and arrange on individual serving plates.

Spoon over the sauce and garnish with the carrots, roast garlic and parsley.

FRESH TARRAGON NOODLES

Note this clever cooking method, which gives a perfect texture for homemade pasta; Dried pasta can be cooked the same way, but bought fresh pasta doesn't give good results.

Pasta:
1 egg plus 1 yolk
1 clove garlic
225 g (8 oz) pasta flour (Italian wheat flour type oo)
3.75 ml (¾ tsp) salt
30-60 ml (1-2 fl oz) water
6 tarragon sprigs, leaves only, chopped
plenty of freshly ground black pepper
semolina flour, for rolling out

To Serve:
large knob of butter

Put the egg, extra yolk and garlic in a food processor and work until frothy. With the machine running, add the flour a spoonful at a time and the salt through the feeder tube. Add the water a little at a time, the mixture should only just stick together, and process 1 minute. Knead in the tarragon and pepper.

Roll out the pasta, cut into three and put each sheet through a pasta machine: gradually roll thinner and thinner until you reach no. 5 (no. 6 being the finest). Put through the noodle slicing attachment.

Bring 3 litres (5 pints) water to the boil in a large saucepan with 30 ml (2 tbsp) salt added. Put in the noodles, boil for 2-3 minutes then turn off the heat, leaving the pasta in the water. Leave for 8-12 minutes, then drain, toss in butter and serve immediately.

Note: If you do not have a pasta machine, roll out the dough as thinly as possible then cut into strips to make noodles.

BUTTER-COOKED LETTUCE

Cooked lettuce has a delicate flavour all of its own – quite unlike any other leaf vegetable.

2 Little Gem or small Cos lettuce
salt and freshly ground black pepper
sugar to taste
15 ml (1 tbsp) butter

Trim each lettuce, slice in half lengthwise and season with salt, pepper and sugar to taste. Heat the butter in a frying pan, add the lettuce and fry very gently, turning occasionally for about 15-20 minutes until each side is browned. Serve immediately.

Fig Tart with Scented Cream

Figs are at their most delicious, bottled and left for a month. Simply blanch them in boiling water for 3 minutes, then drain and bottle in syrup made from 225 g (8 oz) sugar and 600 ml (1 pint) water – the syrup is not to be wasted! My friend Andy Leamon inspired this special and eye-catching recipe.

Pastry:
15 g (½ oz) fine semolina
185 g (6½ oz) flour
5 ml (1 tsp) sugar
1.25 ml (¼ tsp) salt
110 g (4 oz) butter
finely grated rind of ½ orange
1 egg yolk
15 ml (1 tbsp) rosewater
beaten egg white for brushing

Filling:
75 g (3 oz) ground almonds
50 g (2 oz) sugar
65 g (2½ oz) butter, melted
15 ml (1 tbsp) mirabelle (plum eau-de-vie)
15 ml (1 tbsp) cream
1 egg
10 bottled or tinned figs, drained and halved

Glaze:
450 ml (¾ pint) syrup from the figs
juice of 1 lemon, or to taste

Scented Cream:
150 ml (¼ pint) double cream
10 ml (2 tsp) mirabelle (plum eau-de-vie)
10 ml (2 tsp) icing sugar
5 ml (1 tsp) rosewater
5 ml (1 tsp) orange flower water, or to taste

To make the pastry, put the dry ingredients in a food processor with the butter and orange rind and process until the mixture resembles fine breadcrumbs. Add the egg yolk and rosewater through the feeder tube to bind the mixture. Wrap and chill in the refrigerator for 20 minutes.

Roll out the pastry thinly and use to line a 25 cm (10 inch) flan tin. Chill in the refrigerator for 15 minutes, then prick the base with a fork. Brush with egg white, then line with greaseproof paper and baking beans and bake blind in a preheated oven at 190°C (375°F) mark 5 for 15-20 minutes. Remove paper and beans.

To make the filling, in a bowl mix the ground almonds with the sugar. Stir in the melted butter, eau-de-vie, cream and egg. Fill the pastry case with the almond filling and top with the halved figs. Bake in the oven for 20-25 minutes, until set. Allow to cool.

For the glaze, boil the syrup until reduced and thickened, adding lemon juice to taste. Brush over the fig tart.

To make the scented cream, whip the double cream with the eau-de-vie, icing sugar, rosewater and orange flower water to taste.

Serve the fig tart with the scented cream.

*Dark Chocolate Leaves layered with White Chocolate
Mousse in a pool of Vanilla Sauce*

VANESSA BINNS' DESSERT (REGIONAL HEAT)

Pan-fried Duck Breast on a Salad of Braised Red Cabbage
MARK JAMES' STARTER (REGIONAL HEAT)

REGIONAL HEATS
THE SOUTH WEST
ORLANDO MURRIN • JAN GILBERTHORPE • HELEN POTHECARY

JAN GILBERTHORPE'S MENU

STARTER
Smoked Duck Breast with a Carrot and Ginger Salad in Honey Dressing
"THAT IS THE BEST TASTING SMOKED DUCK I HAVE EVER TASTED " LOYD

MAIN COURSE
Fillet of Baby Halibut with Fennel, Shallots and Roasted Red Pepper
New Potatoes
"GREAT SUCCESS" JEAN MARSH
"THE FENNEL GOES SO WELL WITH HALIBUT" LOYD

DESSERT
Walnut and Orange Tartlets with Crème Fraîche
"IT TASTES AS GOOD AS IT SMELLS. A HUGE SUCCESS"
JEAN MARSH

Jan lives in Hewish near Weston-Super-Mare in a large farmhouse which is furnished country-style. She has a 17 year old daughter. She is fond of animals and keeps five sheep and two border terriers. Jan loves gardening and DIY, particularly redecorating and making home furnishings. In her spare time she plays tennis on their own court, and enjoys going to auctions.

SMOKED DUCK BREAST WITH CARROT AND GINGER SALAD IN HONEY DRESSING

Smoked duck breasts can be purchased in some good delicatessens at a price! However, it is a simple and fun task to smoke one's own – either in a commercial smoke box or, as I do, in a home-made brick smoke box in the garden. It is a rather inexact science and timing will depend on your method. I do mine as follows:

2 Barbary duck breasts, each
about 350 g (12 oz)
10 ml (2 tsp) Szechuan peppercorns, crushed
4 spring onions, finely chopped
5 ml (1 tsp) finely grated lime rind
5 ml (1 tsp) sea salt

To Serve:
Carrot and Ginger Salad (see right)

Place the duck breasts in a dish. Mix the peppercorns, spring onions, lime rind and salt together and rub all over the duck breasts. Cover and refrigerate overnight, turning once or twice.

The next day, scrape the marinade off the duck breasts and pat them dry.

Build a fire as you would for a barbecue and, when the coals are glowing hot, throw on 6 tablespoons each of slightly damp sawdust and hickory chips. You should get smoke almost immediately. Put the duck breasts skin side down on a rack about 15 cm (6 inches) above the fire, place a lid on your 'fire-box' and smoke for about 15 minutes. Turn the breasts and smoke for a further 2 minutes or so.

Leave the duck breasts to settle for 20 minutes, then place a weight on top to compress the flesh.

When ready to serve, remove the skin and slice the duck very thinly. Arrange the slices in overlapping circles on four plates and place the carrot and ginger salad in the centre of the duck.

Note: Hickory chips are obtainable from good kitchen shops.

CARROT AND GINGER SALAD WITH HONEY DRESSING

selection of salad leaves, eg frisée, lamb's
lettuce, radicchio
10 ml (2 tsp) finely slivered fresh root ginger
3-4 medium carrots

Dressing:
30 ml (2 tbsp) clear honey
30 ml (2 tbsp) olive oil
15 ml (1 tbsp) lemon juice
salt and freshly ground black pepper

Drop the ginger slivers into a pan of boiling water and boil for 2 minutes. Drain and pat dry. Peel the carrots and cut into sticks 3 x 3 mm x 4 cm (⅛ x ⅛ inch x 1½ inches).

To make the dressing, warm the honey if necessary to thin it out a little, then put it into a screw-topped jar with the oil and lemon juice. Shake to mix, then season with salt and pepper.

Put the carrot and ginger in a bowl and pour over the dressing. Mix well. Place the salad leaves in the centre of the smoked duck slices and top with the carrot mixture.

FILLET OF BABY HALIBUT WITH FENNEL, SHALLOTS AND ROASTED RED PEPPER

1 red pepper
75 g (3 oz) butter
1 fennel bulb, sliced
4 shallots, sliced
salt and freshly ground black pepper
4 skinned baby halibut fillets, each about
125-150 g (4-5 oz)
½ lime
2 spinach leaves

Roast the pepper over an open flame or under a preheated hot grill, turning frequently until it is black all over. Place it in a covered bowl until cool enough to handle, then peel, remove the core and seeds, and dice the flesh.

Heat 50 g (2 oz) butter in a covered pan, add the fennel and shallot slices and soften, without browning, for about 10 minutes. Add the diced pepper, then season with salt and pepper.

Butter 4 pieces of foil, each about 30 x 40 cm (12 x 16 inches). Divide the fennel mixture between them, then top each with a halibut fillet, a squeeze of lime juice, a sprinkling of salt and a knob of butter. Fold the foil to make loose parcels, sealing the edges well.

Place the parcels on a heated baking tray and cook in a preheated oven at 200°C (400°F) mark 6 for 6-8 minutes, depending on the thickness of the fish.

While the fish is cooking, shred the spinach, immerse briefly in boiling water and drain thoroughly.

Place a fillet of fish on each plate, surround with the fennel mixture and top with a few strands of spinach. Serve immediately, accompanied by new potatoes.

WALNUT AND ORANGE TARTLETS

Pastry:
100 g (4 oz) plain flour
pinch of salt
75 g (3 oz) butter
finely grated rind and juice of 1 orange
1 egg yolk

Filling:
2 small eggs, size 4
120 ml (4 fl oz) pure maple syrup
15 g (½ oz) unsalted butter, melted
5 ml (1 tsp) finely grated orange rind
5 ml (1 tsp) pure orange essence
100 g (4 oz) shelled walnuts

To Finish:
300 ml (½ pint) crème fraîche

For the pastry, sift the flour and salt into a bowl and rub in the butter until the mixture resembles breadcrumbs. Stir in 5 ml (1 tsp) finely grated orange rind and mix to a dough with the egg yolk and about 15 ml (1 tbsp) orange juice. Alternatively, prepare the pastry in a food processor. Wrap the pastry and leave to rest in the refrigerator for 30 minutes.

Roll out the pastry on a lightly floured surface and use to line four 10 cm (4 inch) tartlet tins. Leave to rest in the refrigerator for 30 minutes. Prick the bases with a fork. Line with greaseproof paper and baking beans and bake blind in a preheated oven at 200°C (400°F) mark 6 for 8 minutes. Remove the paper and beans.

For the filling, mix together the eggs, maple syrup, unsalted butter, finely grated orange rind and the orange essence.

Reserve 4 nice walnut halves, chop the rest coarsely and divide between the tartlet cases. Pour the orange syrup mixture over the walnuts and cook in a preheated oven at 170°C (325°F) mark 3 for about 25 minutes until puffed and golden brown. Allow to cool.

Meanwhile, pour boiling water onto the reserved walnut halves, leave for 5 minutes, then remove the skins. Roast in a preheated oven at 180°C (350°F) mark 4 for about 5 minutes until golden.

Whip the crème fraîche until it holds soft peaks. Pipe a rosette on to the centre of each cooled tartlet and top with a roasted walnut half. Serve the rest of the crème fraîche separately.

REGIONAL HEATS

THE SOUTH WEST

ORLANDO MURRIN • JAN GILBERTHORPE • HELEN POTHECARY

HELEN POTHECARY'S MENU

STARTER

Crab Parcels and Pink Grapefruit on a Ginger Sauce

MAIN COURSE

Fillet of Venison on a Damson Sauce
Celeriac Baskets
Gratin of Jerusalem Artichokes
Sauté of Spinach and Watercress
"NICELY UNDERSTATED. REALLY SUPERB COMBINATION" LOYD

DESSERT

Crème Caramel with Almond Petits Fours

Helen comes from Belgium and now lives in a charming Dorset cottage with her husband, 10 year old daughter and a sheepdog. She runs her own business dealing in upmarket children's leisurewear. Originally a gym teacher, Helen enjoys most types of sport, including tennis, weights, aerobics and skiing. In calmer moments, she enjoys embroidery and local activities.

CRAB PARCELS AND PINK GRAPEFRUIT ON A GINGER SAUCE

To make these parcels you will need about 4 leeks to obtain 24 leek leaves, each approximately 15 cm (6 inches) long and 5 cm (2 inches) wide. Split each leek in half lengthwise and open out to release the leaves. Don't use the tough outer leaves or the narrow inner leaves.

Parcels:
400 ml (14 fl oz) chicken stock
24 leek leaves

Filling:
15 ml (1 tbsp) unsalted butter
2 shallots, chopped
1 large clove garlic
7 5 ml (1½ tsp) grated fresh root ginger
1 medium dressed crab, white meat only

Sauce:
100 ml (3½ fl oz) dry vermouth
300 ml (½ pint) fish stock
200 ml (7 fl oz) double cream
25 g (1 oz) chilled unsalted butter, diced

To Finish:
1-2 pink grapefruits
chives to garnish

To make the parcels, bring the chicken stock to the boil in a large saucepan, add the leek leaves and blanch for about 30 seconds. Drain on absorbent kitchen paper, then arrange in pairs to form crosses. You should have 12 crosses.

To make the filling, heat the butter in a pan, add the shallots, garlic and ginger and cook until softened. Remove from the heat and set aside half of the mixture for the sauce. Mix the rest with the crabmeat.

Divide the filling between the leeks, placing it in the centre of the crosses. Fold the leek leaves over to enclose the filling and form small parcels.

To make the ginger sauce, place the reserved shallot, garlic and ginger mixture in a saucepan with the vermouth and boil steadily until reduced by half. Add the fish stock and reduce by half again. Strain through a sieve then add the cream and heat through. Finally whisk in the butter, a piece at a time, to obtain a smooth glossy sauce.

Place the crab parcels in a steamer and steam for about 3 minutes or until heated through.

Peel and segment the grapefruit, discarding all pith. Pour the ginger sauce on to individual serving plates and place 3 crab parcels in the centre of each plate. Arrange the grapefruit segments on the plates and garnish with chives. Serve immediately.

FILLET OF VENISON ON A DAMSON SAUCE

If you are able to obtain chinos molle – South American red berries – they add a delicate finishing touch to this dish.

800 g (1¾ lb) venison fillet
20 ml (1½ tbsp) olive oil

Sauce:
500 ml (16 fl oz) venison stock
75 ml (5 tbsp) port
75 ml (5 tbsp) damson juice
about 15 ml (1 tbsp) honey
25 g (1 oz) clarified butter
25 g (1 oz) unsalted cold butter, diced
salt and freshly ground black pepper

To Garnish:
chinos molle berries (optional)

Brush the venison fillet with the olive oil and set aside.

To make the sauce, reduce the venison stock to 400 ml (14 fl oz) then add the port and reduce by a further 100 ml (3½ fl oz). Add the damson juice. The sauce should have a fairly thick consistency; if necessary boil to reduce further. Add honey to taste. Keep warm.

Heat the clarified butter in a frying pan and add the venison fillet. Cook over a high heat, turning constantly for about 7 minutes until sealed and brown on all sides. Keep warm in a low oven at 150°C (300°F) mark 2 while finishing the sauce.

Add the unsalted butter to the sauce, a piece at a time, whisking gently to obtain a glossy finish. Check seasoning.

Slice the venison fillet and fan out on warmed individual plates. Spoon the damson sauce around the meat. Sprinkle a few chinos molle berries on the meat if available. Serve immediately with the vegetable accompaniments.

CELERIAC BASKETS

1 medium celeriac bulb
15 ml (1 tbsp) unsalted butter
45 ml (3 tbsp) double cream
salt and freshly ground black pepper
peanut oil for deep frying

To make the baskets, peel the celeriac and cut into four 4 cm (1½ inch) thick rings. Here comes the tricky bit! Scoop a hollow out of the middle of each celeriac ring about the size of a large egg cup, leaving a firm base. Reserve the scooped out celeriac. Adjust the diameter of the baskets by peeling all round to make them the same size. Immerse in a bowl of cold water until required.

To make the filling, cut the reserved celeriac into 2.5 cm (1 inch) cubes and place in a saucepan. Add water to cover, bring to the boil and simmer until tender. Drain and place in a blender or food processor with the butter and cream. Purée until smooth. Season with salt and pepper to taste.

Heat the peanut oil in a deep-fat fryer and deep-fry the baskets until crisp and golden. Drain on absorbent kitchen paper and fill with the celeriac purée to serve.

GRATIN OF JERUSALEM ARTICHOKES

500 g (1 lb) Jerusalem artichokes
salt and freshly ground black pepper
15 ml (1 tbsp) unsalted butter
300 ml (½ pint) double cream

Slice the Jerusalem artichokes into 5 mm (¼ inch) rings. Season with salt and pepper. Layer the artichoke slices in a buttered gratin dish. Dot with butter and pour over the cream. Cook in a preheated oven at 180°C (350°F) mark 4 for 15-20 minutes until tender.

SAUTÉ OF SPINACH AND WATERCRESS

250 g (9 oz) washed spinach
150 g (5 oz) washed watercress, longer
*   stalks removed*
30 ml (2 tbsp) quality extra virgin olive oil
salt and freshly ground black pepper

Tear the leaves of the spinach and mix with the watercress. Heat the oil in a frying pan and when it is really hot, add the spinach and watercress mixture. Sauté for about 30 seconds only. Season with salt and pepper to taste and serve immediately.

CRÈME CARAMEL

Caramel Sauce:
90 g (3½ oz) caster sugar

Crème:
400 ml (14 fl oz) milk
1 vanilla pod or few drops of vanilla essence
5 egg yolks
80 g (3¼ oz) caster sugar

To prepare the caramel sauce, place the sugar in a saucepan with 15 ml (1 tbsp) hot water. Dissolve over a low heat, then increase the heat and cook until the sauce is the colour of honey but still runny. Pour the caramel into 4 ramjekins; set aside.

To make the crème, pour the milk into a saucepan. Split the vanilla pod if using and extract the seeds. Add these or the vanilla essence to the milk and bring to a gentle simmer. Allow to infuse into the milk. Simmer gently for 4 minutes, but do not overheat.

Whisk the egg yolks and sugar together in a bowl. Gradually whisk in the milk, then pass through a sieve into a clean bowl. Divide the custard equally between the 4 ramekins. Place them in a roasting tin containing enough hot water to come halfway up the sides of the ramekins. Bake in a preheated oven at 170°C (325°F) mark 3 for 45-50 minutes until set. Allow to cool at room temperature for about 30 minutes, then chill in the refrigerator until required.

To serve, run the blade of a knife carefully around the inside of each dish and turn each crème caramel out on to a serving plate. Serve with the almond petits fours.

ALMOND PETITS FOURS

1 egg white
60 g (2¾ oz) ground almonds
30 g (1¼ oz) caster sugar

Whisk the egg white until stiff, then lightly fold in the ground almonds and sugar. Put into a piping bag, fitted with a fluted nozzle, and pipe into small rosette shapes on a baking tray.

Bake in a preheated oven at 170°C (325°F) mark 3 for 10-15 minutes or until golden brown at the edges. Transfer to a wire rack to cool.

REGIONAL HEATS
LONDON
NICHOLAS HOCKING • ROSE GIBSON • NICHOLAS POUND

WINNER

NICHOLAS HOCKING'S MENU

STARTER
Japanese California Roll Sushi
"THE TOTAL TASTE ALTOGETHER IS LOVELY" JOYCE MOLYNEUX
"VERY NICE, I WOULD LIKE ANOTHER BIT" PETER BOWLES

MAIN COURSE
*Marinated Duck Breasts on a bed of Fried Celery with a Lemon
and Caraway Sauce*
Pommes Anna
Gingered Carrot and Courgette Ribbons

DESSERT
Hazelnut Praline Ice Cream on a Raspberry Coulis

Nick is an Australian living in London, and a dentist by profession. He once windsurfed round North Tasmania! From Australia, he moved on to Japan where he worked as a dentist and he speaks fluent Japanese, as well as French. Nick has learnt Judo and Kendo – a Japanese version of sword fighting. He enjoys pottery, waterskiing, clay pigeon shooting, tennis, riding and playing the drums, guitar and piano.

JAPANESE CALIFORNIA ROLL SUSHI

You can vary the ingredients for sushi according to taste and availability. Try using baby courgettes instead of bamboo stalk.

500 g (1 lb 2 oz) short-grain (sushi) rice

Vinegar Mix:
75 ml (5 tbsp) rice wine vinegar
15 ml (1 tbsp) mirin
45 ml (3 tbsp) sugar
5 ml (1 tsp) salt

To Assemble:
2 sheets dried seaweed
½ avocado, peeled and stoned
½ small cucumber
2 strips sweetened bamboo stalk
2 egg yolks, fried until firm
5 ml (1 tsp) roasted sesame seeds
30 ml (2 tbsp) soy sauce
2.5 ml (½ tsp) wasabe (Japanese horseradish)

Cook the rice in boiling salted water for 20 minutes. Turn off the heat and leave, covered, for a further 20 minutes to allow the rice to become slightly sticky. Drain and allow to cool. Combine the ingredients for the vinegar mix, add to the rice and fork through.

Lay the dried seaweed on a work surface and spread the rice on top to a 5 mm (¼ inch) thickness, leaving a 2.5 cm (1 inch) border at the top edge. Cut the avocado, cucumber, bamboo stalk and fried egg yolks into thin strips, then lay on top of the rice.

Transfer the sheet to a bamboo mat. Moisten the top edge of seaweed, then roll tightly from the bottom to enclose the rice mixture. Slice the roll diagonally and sprinkle the slices with toasted sesame seeds.

Serve with soy sauce and a dash of wasabe.

GINGERED CARROT AND COURGETTE RIBBONS

3 carrots
2 courgettes
2.5 ml (½ tsp) finely chopped fresh root ginger
10 ml (2 tsp) sesame oil
salt and freshly ground black pepper

Slice the carrots and courgettes into long, very thin ribbons using a mandoline if possible, discarding the central core of each vegetable.

Heat the oil in a frying pan, add the ginger and sauté for about 30 seconds, then add the carrots and sauté for 30 seconds. Finally, add the courgettes and sauté for a further 30 seconds or until just tender.

Add seasoning and serve immediately in a tangled configuration.

MARINATED DUCK BREASTS ON A BED OF FRIED CELERY WITH A LEMON AND CARAWAY SAUCE

4 duck breasts
2 sticks celery, chopped

Marinade:
juice of ½ lemon
1 clove garlic, chopped
1 bay leaf
½ onion, chopped
1.25 ml (¼ tsp) caraway seeds
250 ml (8 fl oz) dry white wine

Sauce:
500 ml (16 fl oz) chicken stock
1.25 ml (¼ tsp) caraway seeds
15 ml (1 tbsp) dry sherry
salt and freshly ground black pepper
5 ml (1 tsp) sugar
juice of ½ lemon
7.5 ml (½ tsp) chilled unsalted butter, diced

Remove excess fat from the duck breasts and reserve; score the skin using a sharp knife. Mix together the ingredients for the marinade in a large shallow dish. Add the duck breasts and turn to coat in the flavourings, then leave to marinate for about 2 hours.

Heat the reserved fat in a large frying pan to oil the pan, then discard. Add the duck breasts and fry on both sides for 8 minutes then transfer to a roasting tin. Cook in a preheated oven at 220°C (425°F) mark 7 for 20-35 minutes, depending on the size of the duck breasts, until tender. Fry the celery in the juices remaining in the pan until softened, set aside.

Meanwhile to make the sauce, pour the stock into a saucepan and reduce over moderate heat by about half. Add the caraway seeds, sherry, salt and pepper, sugar and lemon juice. Off the heat, gradually whisk in the unsalted butter to yield a glossy sauce.

Serve the duck breasts on a bed of fried celery. Pour over the lemon and caraway sauce and serve with the accompaniments.

POMMES ANNA

½ onion, finely chopped
1 clove garlic, chopped
30 ml (2 tbsp) olive oil
pinch of freshly grated nutmeg
salt and freshly ground black pepper
4-6 potatoes
250 ml (8 fl oz) chicken stock

Sweat the onion and garlic slowly in the olive oil with the nutmeg, salt and pepper until softened.

Thinly slice the potatoes and toss with the onion mixture. Layer the flavoured potato slices in individual ramekins. Pour over the chicken stock.

Cook in a preheated oven at 200°C (400°F) mark 6 for 30 minutes or until al denté (just tender but firm to the bite). Serve with the duck breasts.

HAZELNUT PRALINE ICE CREAM ON A RASPBERRY COULIS

Ice Cream:
100 g (4 oz) shelled hazelnuts
50 g (2 oz) granulated sugar
125 ml (4 fl oz) water
3 egg whites
150 ml (5 fl oz) single cream
90 ml (3 fl oz) double cream
125 g (4½ oz) caster sugar

Coulis:
225 g (8 oz) raspberries
125 ml (4 fl oz) water
juice of ½ lemon
75 g (3 oz) caster sugar

To Decorate:
mint leaves

Toast the hazelnuts in a preheated oven at 180°C (350°F) mark 4 for about 10 minutes until browned.

Dissolve the granulated sugar in the water in a saucepan over a low heat, then increase the heat and cook until caramelised. Remove from the heat, carefully add the hazelnuts, tossing them to coat with caramel, then allow to cool. Work the cold hazelnut mixture in a blender or food processor, until coarsely ground.

Whisk the egg whites until firm. In another bowl, whip the single and double creams together with the caster sugar until just beginning to thicken. Fold the ground hazelnut mixture into the cream mixture, then lightly fold into the egg whites.

Turn into an ice cream machine and churn for 40 minutes, then place in the freezer until required. Alternatively, pour the mixture into a freezerproof container and freeze until semi-frozen; whisk the mixture and return to the freezer until firm.

To prepare the coulis, put the raspberries in a saucepan with the water, lemon juice and sugar. Heat gently until the sugar has dissolved, then simmer gently until the mixture is reduced by one third. Purée the mixture in a blender or food processor, then sieve to remove the pips.

To serve, pour the raspberry coulis on to individual serving plates and top with the ice cream. Decorate with mint leaves to serve.

REGIONAL HEATS
LONDON
NICHOLAS HOCKING • ROSE GIBSON • NICHOLAS POUND

ROSE GIBSON'S MENU

STARTER

Rendezvous of Prawns and Mushrooms

MAIN COURSE

Spiced Pork Tenderloin

Palusami

Cardamom Rice with Lime

"THE PALUSAMI'S GOT A REAL KICK TO IT" LOYD

DESSERT

Hazelnut Tarts with Mango Coulis

Rose is married and lives in London. She is a director of a PR company, responsible for in-house and external courses. She read English at Oxford and used to be a theatre critic before going into public relations. Rose enjoys organising serious wine tasting sessions and is contemplating trying for a master wine taster's certificate. Her general interests include the theatre, cinema and sport, and she is currently learning to play golf.

RENDEZVOUS OF PRAWN AND MUSHROOM

450 g (1 Ib) raw king prawns in shell
30 ml (2 tbsp) sunflower oil
5 cloves garlic, shredded
1 bunch spring onions, shredded
2 green chillies, shredded
4 kaffir lime leaves (optional)
25 g (1 oz) butter
salt and freshly ground black pepper
125 g (4 oz) mushrooms, preferably shitake, sliced

Dressing:
45 ml (3 tbsp) lime juice
grated rind of 1 lime
dash of 'Nam Pla' fish sauce
5 ml (1 tsp) sugar

To Serve:
frisée
radicchio
chopped coriander leaves to garnish

Shell the prawns and devein, then set aside.

Heat 15 ml (1 tbsp) oil in a frying pan. Add the garlic and fry until crisp and just beginning to turn brown, then remove with a slotted spoon and drain on absorbent kitchen paper. Add the spring onions to the pan and cook until turning brown and crisp; remove and set aside. Repeat with the chillies and kaffir lime leaves if using.

To make the dressing, in a small bowl, mix the lime juice with the grated rind, fish sauce and sugar; set aside.

Melt the butter with the remaining 15 ml (1 tbsp) oil in the frying pan over moderate heat, add the prawns and toss until pink, then remove with a slotted spoon. Drain and place in a bowl. Season with pepper.

Add the mushrooms to the fat remaining in the pan and cook over a high heat until softened. Remove and toss together with the prawns. Pour over the lime dressing and toss again.

To serve, arrange frisée and radicchio leaves on individual serving plates. Quickly toss the deep-fried aromatics with the prawns and mushrooms, then divide between the plates. Scatter with chopped coriander and serve.

SPICED PORK TENDERLOIN

4 pork tenderloin fillets

Marinade:
60 ml (4 tbsp) chopped parsley
30 ml (2 tbsp) Mexican chilli powder
6 cloves garlic, crushed
15 ml (1 tbsp) cumin seeds
15 ml (1 tbsp) ground coriander
5 ml (1 tsp) ground cinnamon
200 ml (7 fl oz) red wine
30 ml (2 tbsp) red wine vinegar
generous pinch each of chopped oregano,
  basil and thyme

Sauce:
225 g (8 oz) butter
500 ml (16 fl oz) cold water
3 tomatoes, chopped
generous pinch of sugar
salt and freshly ground black pepper

Using the tip of a knife, make pinpricks in the pork fillets all over. Mix together the ingredients for the marinade in a shallow dish, then add the pork and turn to coat with the mixture. Leave to marinate for at least 1 hour, then drain, reserving the marinade for the sauce.

Place the pork fillets on a baking tray and cook on the top shelf of a preheated oven at 190°C (375°F) mark 5, for about 30 minutes.

To make the sauce, melt the butter in a saucepan, then add the reserved marinade, water, chopped tomatoes and sugar. Bring to a gentle boil and reduce until the sauce is slightly thickened and rich brown in colour; this will take about 20 minutes. Adjust the seasoning.

Slice the pork fillets and arrange on warmed individual plates. Spoon over the sauce. Serve immediately with the palusami and cardamom rice.

PALUSAMI

Dasheen leaves are available from West Indian food stores, but if you cannot obtain them use 1 kg (2 lb) spinach leaves instead.

2 bundles dasheen leaves
2 medium onions, finely grated
grated rind of 2 lemons
1 plump green chilli, finely chopped
2 cloves garlic, finely chopped
salt
225 g (8 oz) packet frozen coconut cream,
  defrosted

First, prepare the dasheen leaves. Tear off and discard the tip of each leaf and cut off the stems to avoid "itchy throat". Reserve 3 large leaves. Pull the remaining leaves away from their tough veins and shred them.

Line a deep-sided pie dish with foil to create a 'bowl', allowing sufficient overhanging the sides to seal the top. Line this bowl with the reserved dasheen leaves. Scatter one third of the shredded leaves into the 'bowl' followed by half the chopped onions, lemon rind, chopped chilli and garlic. Sprinkle with a little salt. Repeat the layers, ending with a layer of shredded dasheen leaves.

Carefully pour coconut cream over the layers until it comes to the top of the 'bowl'. Pull the overhanging foil tightly together into a 'chimney' and seal completely. Bake in a preheated oven at 190°C (375°F) mark 5 for 1½ hours.

Turn the palusami out and remove the foil. Cut into slices to serve.

CARDAMOM RICE WITH LIME

175 g (6 oz) basmati rice
generous pinch of salt
6 cardamom pods
1.25 ml (¼ tsp) freshly grated turmeric, or
*   turmeric powder*
½ lime

Put the rice in a saucepan with the salt,
cardamom and turmeric. Push the lime
half into the rice. Add sufficient water to
come about 4 cm (1½ inches) above the
level of the rice and bring to the boil.
Lower the heat, cover and simmer for
10-15 minutes. Turn off the heat and
leave covered for a further 5 minutes,
then remove the lime and fluff up the
rice with a fork to serve.

HAZELNUT TARTS WITH MANGO COULIS

Pastry:
250 g (9 oz) plain flour
pinch of salt
100 g (3½ oz) butter, diced
125 g (4 oz) icing sugar
1 egg, size 2

Filling:
90 ml (3 fl oz) golden syrup
50 g (2 oz) butter, melted
2 eggs, size 4, beaten
7.5 ml (1½ tsp) plain flour
75 g (3 oz) brown sugar
150 g (5 oz) shelled hazelnuts, coarsely
*   ground*
generous pinch of ground cinnamon

Mango Coulis:
25 g (1 oz) caster sugar
125 ml (4 fl oz) water
1 mango
lemon juice to taste

To Serve:
150 ml (¼ pint) double cream
icing sugar for dusting

To make the pastry, sift the flour and
salt on to a cool work surface and make
a well in the centre. Add the diced
butter, icing sugar and egg to the well.
Mix these ingredients together, then
gradually work in the flour, using your
hands until a small ball of dough is
formed. Wrap and leave to rest in the
refrigerator for at least 1 hour.

To prepare the filling, mix the golden
syrup with the melted butter. Gradually
whisk the beaten eggs into the syrup
mixture, followed by the flour and
brown sugar. Finally, fold in the ground
hazelnuts and cinnamon.

Roll out the pastry thinly on a lightly
floured surface and use to line four
individual tartlet tins. Spoon in the
filling and shake the tins to level the
mixture. Bake below the middle of a
preheated oven at 180°C (350°F) mark 4
for 1 hour or until the top is set and the
pastry is golden.

Meanwhile, prepare the mango coulis.
Dissolve the sugar in the water in a
saucepan over low heat, then bring to
the boil and boil steadily to make a
clear, sorbet syrup. Peel and chop the
mango, discarding the stone. Purée in a
blender or food processor with the
syrup until smooth. Add lemon juice to
taste.

To serve, transfer the cooked tarts to
individual serving plates. Pour a semi-
circle of coulis on one side of each tart
and a semi-circle of double cream on the
other. Dust with icing sugar and serve
immediately.

REGIONAL HEATS
LONDON
NICHOLAS HOCKING • ROSE GIBSON • NICHOLAS POUND

NICHOLAS POUND'S MENU

STARTER
Parsnip and Coriander Soup

MAIN COURSE
Vegetable, Fruit and Nut Samosas served with a Citrus Sauce
Potato and Cauliflower Bhaji
Pumpkin and Pineapple Chutney
Chick Pea Salad in Coconut Dressing
"I WILL GO TO A RESTAURANT AND ORDER A BOWL OF CHUTNEY IN FUTURE" PETER BOWLES

DESSERT
*Double Chocolate Terrine in a Strawberry Cream
Coulis*
"VERY WICKED INDEED" LOYD

Nicholas lives in London and is an actor by profession, involved in musicals. He read French at university, taught at Bordeaux University for a year, then attended drama school. He subsequently toured with a children's theatre, and later gained parts in 'South Pacific', 'Evita' and 'Chess'. He recently played in a new musical about Florence Nightingale which toured the provinces. Nicholas collects masks from China, Venice, Africa and England. He also enjoys browsing antique markets, and has a passion for Noel Coward.

PARSNIP AND CORIANDER SOUP

45 ml (3 tbsp) olive oil
1 medium onion, finely chopped
2 cloves garlic, finely chopped
700 g (1½ lb) parsnips, peeled and diced
5 ml (1 tsp) turmeric
5 ml (1 tsp) ground cinnamon
30 ml (2 tbsp) chopped fresh coriander leaves
5 ml (1 tsp) ground coriander
1.2 litres (2 pints) vegetable stock
salt and freshly ground black pepper
120 ml (4 fl oz) creamed coconut

To Finish:
desiccated coconut for sprinkling
40 ml (8 tsp) natural yogurt
coriander leaves

Heat the oil in a large saucepan and fry the onion and garlic for a few minutes until tender. Add the parsnips, turmeric, cinnamon, chopped coriander leaves and ground coriander. Cook for 2 minutes, stirring all the time to ensure that the parsnips are thoroughly coated in all the flavourings.

Add the vegetable stock and bring to the boil. Cover and simmer for about 10-15 minutes until the parsnips are tender.

Remove from the heat and purée in a blender or food processor until smooth. Season well. Return the soup to the pan and stir in the creamed coconut over a low heat.

Serve in individual bowls, sprinkled with desiccated coconut. Swirl 10 ml (2 tsp) natural yogurt on to each portion and sprinkle with coriander leaves to serve.

VEGETABLE, FRUIT AND NUT SAMOSAS

2 large carrots, sliced
1 orange
30 ml (2 tbsp) olive oil
1 medium onion, chopped
5 ml (1 tsp) ground coriander
5 ml (1 tsp) ground cinnamon
5 ml (1 tsp) ground cardamom seeds
2 large courgettes, sliced
50 g (2 oz) raisins
25 g (1 oz) chopped hazelnuts
25 g (1 oz) chopped walnuts
15 ml (1 tbsp) desiccated coconut
25-50 g (1-2 oz) ground almonds
90 ml (3 fl oz) orange juice (approximately)
salt and freshly ground black pepper
4 sheets of filo pastry
melted butter for brushing
15-30 ml (1-2 tbsp) flaked almonds

Citrus Sauce:
1 large orange
juice of 1 lemon
300 ml (½ pint) fresh orange juice
2.5 ml (½ tsp) ground cardamom seeds
2.5 ml (½ tsp) ground cinnamon
sugar, to taste
15 ml (1 tbsp) Cointreau (optional)
1.25 ml (¼ tsp) arrowroot

To Garnish:
finely shredded orange and lemon rind
chopped pistachio nuts
coriander leaves

Steam the carrots for about 5 minutes; they should still be crisp. Peel and segment the orange, discarding all pith and pips; chop the flesh.

Heat the oil in a saucepan and fry the onion for a few minutes. Add the spices and heat through. Add the steamed carrots and courgettes and cook for 1 minute, stirring continuously.

Add the orange, raisins, chopped nuts, coconut, ground almonds and orange juice. The mixture should hold together; if it is too dry add a little more juice; if too liquid add more ground almonds. Stir well to thoroughly mix all the ingredients together, then season with salt and pepper to taste.

Cut each sheet of filo pastry into quarters, then fold each quarter in half lengthwise to give 4 strips. Brush each strip with melted butter. Lay 4 filo pastry strips over each of 4 ramekins, crossing them to form a Union Jack pattern and allowing the strips to overlap the edge. Push the pastry down inside the ramekins to line the base and sides. Fill each well with samosa mixture and fold the pastry flaps over the top.

Turn the samosas out of the ramekins on to a greased baking sheet. Brush with melted butter and top with flaked almonds. Bake in a preheated oven at 190°C (375°F) mark 5 for about 20 minutes or until the pastry and almonds are golden brown.

Meanwhile, make the citrus sauce. Peel and segment the orange, discarding all pith and pips; chop the flesh. Put the chopped orange, fruit juices and spices in a saucepan and bring to the boil. Remove from the heat and liquidize, using a blender.

Gradually stir in sugar to taste, then return to the heat and bring to a simmer. Add the Cointreau if using. Blend the arrowroot with a little water, then add to the sauce. Cook, stirring, until slightly thickened.

Place the samosas on warmed serving plates and pour the sauce around. Sprinkle the sauce with orange and lemon rind, and pistachio nuts. Garnish with coriander leaves.

POTATO AND CAULIFLOWER BHAJI

450 g (1 lb) potatoes
25 g (1 oz) butter or margarine
1 large onion, sliced into rings
2 cloves garlic, chopped
15 ml (1 tbsp) minced fresh chilli pepper
10 ml (2 tsp) ground cumin
10 ml (2 tsp) ground coriander
10 ml (2 tsp) garam masala
1 small cauliflower, divided into florets
salt and freshly ground black pepper
30 ml (2 tbsp) olive oil

Peel the potatoes, then grate them into a bowl of cold water. Melt the butter or margarine in a non-stick frying pan and gently fry the onion and garlic until softened. Add the chilli, and 5 ml (1 tsp) each of cumin, coriander and garam masala. Heat through, stirring, for 1 minute, then remove from the heat.

Drain the grated potato and squeeze out excess liquid using your hands. Add to the frying pan and stir to coat in the spices. Return to a low heat.

Slice the cauliflower florets lengthwise; set aside 12 flat floret shapes. Roughly chop the rest of the cauliflower slices and add them to the potato mixture. Stir well, then flatten the mixture, using the back of a wooden spoon, to form an omelette shape. Season well.

Cook the bhaji for 5-10 minutes on each side until golden brown; keep pressing it down with the back of the spoon so that it cooks right through.

In another pan, fry the remaining spices in the olive oil for about 1 minute, then add the reserved cauliflower floret shapes and cook until golden brown.

Either slice the bhaji into quarters in the pan or transfer to a baking sheet and cut out 8 rounds, using a plain pastry cutter. Arrange the fried cauliflower florets on top of the bhaji to serve.

PUMPKIN AND PINEAPPLE CHUTNEY

1 small onion, chopped
175 g (6 oz) pumpkin, diced
225 g (8 oz) can pineapple chunks in natural
   juice
5 ml (1 tsp) ground cinnamon
5 ml (1 tsp) ground ginger
10 ml (2 tsp) chopped fresh coriander leaves
250 ml (8 fl oz) wine or cider vinegar
1 vegetable stock cube, crumbled
30 ml (2 tbsp) brown sugar
50 g (2 oz) raisins

To Garnish:
chopped pistachio nuts

Place all the ingredients, except the raisins, in a saucepan. Bring to the boil, cover and simmer for 30 minutes or until the pumpkin is very tender.

Remove from the heat and work briefly, using a blender or food processor; the chutney should retain some chunky pieces. Stir in the raisins.

With a slotted spoon, ladle the chutney into a serving bowl, then chill until needed. Serve sprinkled with chopped pistachios.

CHICK PEA SALAD IN COCONUT DRESSING

450 g (1 lb) cooked chick peas

Dressing:
250 ml (8 fl oz) creamed coconut
150 ml (5 fl oz) natural yogurt
15 ml (1 tbsp) finely chopped coriander
   leaves
10 ml (2 tsp) clear honey
30 ml (2 tbsp) desiccated coconut
5 ml (1 tsp) mustard
pinch of salt
pinch of cayenne pepper

To Garnish:
coriander sprigs

Place the chick peas in a serving bowl. Combine the ingredients for the dressing in a jug. Stir well, then pour over the chick peas and toss well. Chill before serving, garnished with coriander sprigs.

Note: Either use canned creamed coconut, which is available from some healthfood shops and delicatessens, or a block of creamed coconut and follow packet directions for use.

DOUBLE CHOCOLATE TERRINE IN A STRAWBERRY CREAM COULIS

White Chocolate Layer:
100 g (4 oz) white chocolate
100 g (4 oz) tofu
50 g (2 oz) unsalted butter
50 g (2 oz) caster sugar
25 g (1 oz) ground almonds
few drops of vanilla essence
15 ml (1 tbsp) whipped cream

Dark Chocolate Layer:
100 g (4 oz) plain chocolate
50 g (2 oz) unsalted butter
50 g (2 oz) caster sugar
100 g (4 oz) unsweetened chestnut purée
25 g (1 oz) ground hazelnuts
30 ml (2 tbsp) brandy

To Assemble:
*1 packet langue de chat biscuits or Barmouth
    biscuits*
brandy for soaking

Coulis:
400 g (14 oz) strawberries in syrup
90 ml (3 fl oz) double cream

To Decorate:
4 fresh strawberries, sliced

First make the white chocolate mixture. Break the chocolate into pieces and place in a heatproof bowl over a saucepan of hot water until melted.

Meanwhile, mince the tofu in a food processor or blender. Cream together the butter and sugar in a mixing bowl until light and fluffy. Add the minced tofu, ground almonds, vanilla essence and whipped cream. Beat thoroughly. Add the melted chocolate and beat well.

Dip some of the biscuits into the brandy, then use to line the base and sides of a 450 g (1 lb) loaf tin. Pour in enough white chocolate mixture to half-fill the loaf tin. Chill in the refrigerator until firm.

To make the dark chocolate mixture, break the chocolate into pieces and melt in a heatproof bowl over a saucepan of hot water. In a mixing bowl, cream together the butter and sugar until light and fluffy. Add the chestnut purée, ground hazelnuts and brandy. Beat thoroughly, then beat in the melted chocolate. Pour the dark chocolate mixture over the white chocolate. Top with a layer of brandy-soaked biscuits. Chill in the refrigerator until firm.

To make the coulis, simply purée the strawberries with their syrup and the cream in a blender or food processor.

To serve, turn out the terrine onto a board and cut into 4 slices. Arrange each slice in the centre of a serving plate. Pour the strawberry coulis around the terrine. Decorate with strawberries.

REGIONAL HEATS

THE NORTH

LINDA YEWDALL • MICHELLE HATTEE • TIM ROBINSON

WINNER

LINDA YEWDALL'S MENU

STARTER

Hot Smoked Wild Salmon Sauce on a Green Salad

"THE SMOKINESS IS LOVELY IN THE SAUCE. I COULD GO ON AND ON EATING IT" JOSCELINE DIMBLEBY

"STRONG EVOCATIVE TASTE" JOHN HARVEY-JONES

MAIN COURSE

Oxtail in Port with Root Vegetables and Hedgerow Jelly
Bubble and Squeak Parcels

"YUMMY" JOSCELINE DIMBLEBY

"JUST HEAVEN WITH BUBBLE AND SQUEAK – GOSH THAT'S GOOD" LOYD

DESSERT

Baked Bramleys with Cobnut Stuffing and Cardamom Custard

"A BRILLIANT CONCEPT" JOHN HARVEY-JONES

"A SUBLIME DISH" LOYD

In her mid-30's Linda left a conventional life in Tunbridge Wells to become self-sufficient and live a hand-to-mouth existence in a Scottish cottage for five years. She then moved to Yorkshire where she married. Linda and her husband now have a small holding with 64 dairy cows, as well as pigs and sheepdogs. As a hobby, Linda continues to spin, a craft she used to earn her living from in Scotland. She has also fulfilled a childhood dream and bought an Austin Seven which she is lovingly restoring.

HOT SMOKED WILD SALMON SAUCE ON A GREEN SALAD

50 g (1¾ oz) can anchovies in oil
300 ml (½ pint) double cream
5 ml (1 tsp) tomato purée
freshly ground black pepper
a little finely chopped parsley
125 g (4 oz) smoked wild salmon, cut into
   ribbons

Salad:

assorted salad leaves 'with bite', eg chicory,
   watercress, frisée
few spring onions
handful of mangetout, finely sliced
few tarragon leaves
lime juice to taste
small handful each of green and pink
   peppercorns in brine, drained

Drain the anchovies, reserving the oil. Place half of them in a heavy-based saucepan with the anchovy oil. Cook over a low heat, stirring with a wooden spoon, to make a smooth paste. Add the cream and tomato purée, stirring until the mixture bubbles. Continue cooking over a low heat, stirring occasionally, until a thick sauce is formed.

Add pepper to taste and a tiny amount of finely chopped parsley. Set aside a few of the smoked salmon ribbons for garnish; add the rest to the sauce.

Combine the salad leaves, spring onions, mangetout and tarragon leaves in a bowl. Sprinkle with lime juice and pepper to taste. Arrange the salad in individual bowls and dot with green and pink peppercorns. Sprinkle with the reserved ribbons of salmon.

Pour the hot sauce over the salad and serve immediately.

OXTAIL IN PORT WITH ROOT VEGETABLES AND HEDGEROW JELLY

1.5 kg (3 lb) oxtail
2 onions, sliced
150 ml (¼ pint) port
2 bay leaves
15 ml (1 tbsp) tomato purée
grated rind and juice of 1 orange
juice of 1 lime
1.2 litres (2 pints) oxtail stock (see below)
salt and freshly ground black pepper
225 g (8 oz) carrots, sliced
225 g (8 oz) parsnips, sliced
2 sticks celery, sliced
1 leek, sliced
15 ml (1 tbsp) hedgerow jelly

To Serve:
chopped parsley to garnish
Hedgerow Jelly (see right)

Trim the fat from the oxtail and seal in a hot heavy-based saucepan, without additional fat, on all sides. Remove and set aside. Fry the onions in the fat remaining in the pan until softened, then remove. Deglaze the pan with half of the port, stirring to scrape up the sediment.

Place the onions, oxtail, meat juices, bay leaves, tomato purée, fruit juices, stock and seasoning in a pressure cooker and cook for 45 minutes (see note).

Transfer to a flameproof casserole and mop up excess fat from the surface with absorbent kitchen paper. Add the carrots, parsnips, celery and leek with 15 ml (1 tbsp) hedgerow jelly. Add a little more stock if necessary. Cover and cook in a preheated oven at 180°C (350°F) mark 4 for about 45 minutes to 1 hour. Check the seasoning. Add the remaining port and reduce until the sauce has thickened slightly, on top of the cooker.

Serve sprinkled with parsley and accompanied by hedgerow jelly, and bubble and squeak parcels.

Note: If you do not have a pressure cooker, put the oxtail and flavourings straight into a casserole and cook in a preheated oven at 190°C (375°F) mark 5 for 1½-2 hours before adding the vegetables and continuing as above.

Oxtail Stock: Use the thinner tail ends, with fat removed, to make this. Place in a large pan with a few flavouring vegetables, ie onions, leeks, carrots, and a bouquet garni. Add water to cover, bring to the boil and skim the surface. Cover and simmer gently for 2-3 hours. Alternatively cook in a pressure cooker for just 30 minutes.

HEDGEROW JELLY

Prepare this jelly in the autumn when sloes and crab apples are plentiful and use as required throughout the year. Pick the sloes when they are fully ripe - usually in October.

1 kg (2 lb) crab apples
1 kg (2 lb) sloes, stalks removed
1.2 litres (2 pints) water
sugar (see method)

Chop the crab apples, without peeling or removing the cores. Place the crab apples and sloes in a preserving pan with the water. Bring slowly to the boil, then simmer for about 1 hour. Ladle the fruit and juice into a scalded jelly bag over a bowl and leave to drip through for several hours.

Measure the juice and return to the preserving pan. Add 450 g (1 lb) sugar to each 600 ml (1 pint) juice. Stir over a low heat until the sugar has dissolved, then bring to the boil. Boil rapidly until setting point is reached; this will take approximately 10 minutes. Skim any froth from the surface, then immediately pot in hot sterilized jars.

Note: To save time, cook the fruit in a pressure cooker, it will take just 10 minutes.

BUBBLE AND SQUEAK PARCELS

Savoy cabbage leaves have an interesting texture and they are ideal for these parcels. I use a little of the trimmed fat from the oxtail to fry the vegetable cakes.

4 medium potatoes, cut into even chunks
½ swede, cut into even chunks
175 g (6 oz) broccoli florets
75 g (3 oz) cabbage, shredded
3 spring onions, chopped
salt and freshly ground black pepper
freshly grated nutmeg
oil or fat for frying
4 cabbage leaves
4 spinach leaves
melted butter for brushing

Steam the potatoes and swede (or cook in boiling salted water) until tender, then drain and mash until smooth. Steam the broccoli and cabbage lightly, then chop finely. Combine these vegetables with the spring onions and season with salt, pepper and nutmeg.

Form the mixture into 8 even-sized cakes. Heat a little oil or fat in a frying pan and lightly fry the vegetable cakes on both sides. Remove and drain.

Blanch the cabbage in boiling water for 4 minutes; immediately plunge into cold water to retain the colour, then drain and pat dry with absorbent kitchen paper. Remove the tough stalks. Repeat with the spinach leaves but blanch for 30 seconds only.

Wrap the vegetable cakes in the spinach and cabbage leaves to enclose. Place in a well buttered dish and brush with melted butter. Cover with greaseproof paper and bake in a preheated oven at 170°C (325°F) mark 3 for about 20 minutes.

BAKED BRAMLEYS WITH COBNUT STUFFING

If you are lucky enough to get Kentish cobnuts, use them in preference to hazelnuts for the stuffing.

4 even-sized British Bramley cooking apples
100 g (4 oz) cobnuts or hazelnuts
100 g (4 oz) light muscovado sugar
1 egg yolk
juice of 1 orange
150 ml (¼ pint) sweet cider
knob of butter
sugar for sprinkling

To Serve:
apple leaves and blossom to decorate
   (optional)
Cardamom Custard (see right)

Core the apples, retaining the stalks. Score the skin around the middle of each one.

Grind half of the nuts in a blender or food processor. Roughly chop the other half of the nuts and roast in a preheated oven at 180°C (350°F) mark 4 for about 10 minutes. Combine the ground and roasted nuts with the sugar, egg yolk and orange juice.

Stuff the apples with the nut mixture, then place in a baking dish. Pour the cider around the apples and add a knob of butter and a sprinkling of sugar. Cook in the oven for 45 minutes to 1 hour, depending on the size of the apples, basting occasionally with the juices.

To serve, pop in the reserved stalks and smooth the wrinkled apple skins. Decorate each one with an apple leaf and some apple blossom if the season's right! Serve the baked apples in a pool of cardamom custard.

CARDAMOM CUSTARD

600 ml (1 pint) full-cream milk
50 g (2 oz) sugar
6 cardamom pods
4 egg yolks, beaten

Combine the milk and sugar in a saucepan. Crush the cardamom pods and add to the pan. Heat the milk until it is almost boiling, cool slightly, then pour on to the egg yolks, stirring constantly.

Return to the pan and cook over a low heat, stirring continuously, until the mixture is thick enough to just coat the back of the spoon.

Cover the surface with a piece of greaseproof paper to prevent a skin forming and leave to infuse for about 1 hour. Strain the mixture into a clean pan and reheat gently to serve.

REGIONAL HEATS
THE NORTH
LINDA YEWDALL • MICHELLE HATTEE • TIM ROBINSON

MICHELLE HATTEE'S MENU

STARTER
Poached Local Cod with Fresh Spinach and Melted Butter
"THAT IS SENSATIONAL. VERY INSPIRED COMBINATION"
JOHN HARVEY-JONES

MAIN COURSE
Fillet of Venison infused with Kumquats
Roast Parsnips flavoured with Honey
Steamed Kale
Glazed Carrots and Swede

DESSERT
White Chocolate and Praline Cheesecake with
Caramelised Fruits

Michelle lives in Yorkshire and is in her final year of a BTec Diploma course in Hotel Catering and Management. On leaving school she worked in a local plastics factory, then as a kitchen assistant in a nursing home where she discovered her interest in cooking. Michelle's other interests include painting little china trinket bowls with flowers. In the evenings she helps out at a local pub.

POACHED LOCAL COD WITH FRESH SPINACH AND MELTED BUTTER

450 g (1 lb) cod fillet, skin removed
300 ml (½ pint) fish stock or water
30 ml (2 tbsp) dry white wine
2 lemon slices
small handful of fresh herbs, eg parsley, dill, coriander, basil, thyme, chervil, tarragon
salt and freshly ground black pepper
100 g (4 oz) spinach leaves
100 g (4 oz) unsalted butter

To Garnish:
fresh herbs
lemon slices (optional)

Cut the fish into 4 even-sized portions. Place in a small roasting tin. Pour in the stock or water, add the white wine and arrange the lemon slices and the herbs around the fish. Season with a little salt and pepper, cover with foil and cook in a preheated oven at 190°C (375°F) mark 5 for about 8 minutes until the fish is cooked.

Meanwhile blanch the spinach leaves in boiling water for 3 seconds only. Drain thoroughly and arrange the leaves attractively on individual serving plates. Heat the butter gently in a pan until it turns golden brown in colour.

To serve, place a fish fillet on each plate and pour the butter over the fish. Garnish with the reserved herbs and some lemon slices if you wish.

FILLET OF VENISON INFUSED WITH KUMQUATS

700 g (1½ lb) venison fillet
small handful of herbs, eg parsley, thyme, sage, bay leaf, rosemary
12 kumquats
50 g (2 oz) unsalted butter
½ glass good quality full-bodied red wine
900 ml (1½ pints) venison stock
15 ml (1 tbsp) cornflour
salt and freshly ground black pepper
25 g (1 oz) chilled unsalted butter, diced (optional)

Cut the venison into 4 even-sized strips. Tie the herbs together to make a bouquet garni, reserving a few for garnish. Cut eight of the kumquats into quarters and tie in a piece of muslin cloth in a similar fashion to the bouquet garni.

Melt the butter in a sauté pan and seal the venison on all sides, over a high heat for about 2 minutes. Transfer the venison fillets to a roasting tin and finish cooking in a preheated oven at 190°C (375°F) mark 5 for about 8 minutes.

To make the sauce, pour the red wine into the sauté pan and scrape up the cooking juices. Reduce the wine right down until hardly any liquid remains. Add the stock and reduce by half. Add the bouquet garni and the kumquats in muslin and continue to reduce the liquid until you have about 300 ml (½ pint). Discard the bouquet garni and kumquats. Blend the cornflour with a little water and stir into the sauce to thicken. Season and whisk in the butter if an enriched sauce is preferred.

To serve slice the venison thinly. Pour a little of the sauce into the centre of each plate, and arrange the venison slices on top. Garnish with the reserved herbs and kumquats. Serve with honey flavoured roast parsnips, steamed kale or broccoli and glazed carrots and swede.

WHITE CHOCOLATE AND PRALINE CHEESECAKE WITH CARAMELISED FRUITS

Praline:
60 ml (4 tbsp) granulated sugar
60 ml (4 tbsp) water
50 g (2 oz) toasted chopped nuts

Base:
5 digestive biscuits
25 g (1 oz) unsalted butter

Cheesecake Mixture:
100 g (4 oz) white chocolate
2 leaves gelatine
grated rind and juice of 2 limes
50 g (2 oz) fromage frais
1 egg, separated

Caramelised Fruits:
2 Granny Smith apples
2 Comice pears
3 plums (if available)
125 ml (4 fl oz) orange juice
50 g (2 oz) unsalted butter
75 ml (5 tbsp) caster sugar

To make the praline, dissolve the sugar in the water in a heavy-based pan over low heat, then increase the heat and boil until it turns a caramel colour. Quickly add the nuts and tip the mixture onto a baking tray lined with greaseproof paper. Allow to cool and set hard. Break the praline into pieces and coarsely grind in a food processor or blender. Set aside.

To make the base, put the biscuits in the food processor or blender and process until they resemble fine breadcrumbs. Melt the butter in a pan and add the crushed biscuits. Mix well, then divide between 4 individual loose-based tins, 6-7.5 cm (2½-3 inches) in diameter and 4 cm (1½ inches) deep. Press the crumb mixture down firmly with your fingers. Chill in the refrigerator to harden.

For the cheesecake mixture, carefully melt the white chocolate in a small heatproof bowl over a pan of hot but not boiling water. Meanwhile soak the gelatine leaves in cold water to cover. Allow the melted chocolate to cool slightly. Squeeze the gelatine leaves to remove excess liquid. Gently heat the lime juice in a small pan and stir in the soaked gelatine. In a bowl mix the fromage frais with the egg yolk and 50 g (2 oz) ground praline. Stir in the chocolate lime mixture. Whisk the egg white until it forms soft peaks, then fold into the cheesecake mixture. Spoon the mixture evenly over the bases and chill for 1-2 hours until firm.

Meanwhile prepare the fruits in caramel. Peel, core and slice the apples and pears; quarter the plums and remove the stones if using. Measure the orange juice in a jug. Heat a medium-sized pan and when it starts to get hot, add the apples, pears, butter and sugar. Cook over a high heat until the fruit starts to caramelise, then add the plums and continue to cook until all the fruit is brown and the caramel sauce is rich in colour. Carefully add the orange juice a little at a time until the sauce reaches the desired consistency.

To serve, carefully ease the cheese-cakes out of their tins and place on individual plates. Serve with the warm or cooled caramelised fruits.

Note: If you are unable to find individual loose-bottomed tins, simply use metal rings, 6-7.5 cm (2½-3 inches) in diameter, placed on a baking sheet.

REGIONAL HEATS
The North
Linda Yewdall • Michelle Hattee • Tim Robinson

Tim Robinson's Menu

Starter
Pressed Prawns with Cumin served with Asparagus
"I THINK THE CUMIN IS A REALLY GOOD IDEA. IT WORKS REALLY WELL"
LOYD

Main Course
Piquant Chicken with Coriander and Lime Sauces
Spiced Brown and Wild Rice
Glazed French Beans
Carrots

Dessert
*White Chocolate Ice Cream on a Dark Chocolate and
Hazelnut base with a Raspberry Sauce*

Tim is a curate at St. Mary's church in Acklam. Married with two children, he studied music and drama at Middlesex Polytechnic, worked for a charity, then taught piano, organ and singing for 4 years. With a leaning towards the church he was accepted for training towards ordination at St. Stephen's House in Oxford. Tim is very much a community man. He enjoys playing the organ and singing.

PRESSED PRAWNS WITH CUMIN SERVED WITH ASPARAGUS

25 g (1 oz) unsalted butter
5 ml (1 tsp) cumin seeds, freshly ground
finely grated rind of 1 lemon
625 g (1 lb 5 oz) prawns
juice of ½ lemon
15 ml (1 tbsp) garam masala
150 ml (¼ pint) single cream
12 asparagus spears, trimmed

Melt the butter in a large frying pan until it begins to bubble a little. Add the cumin and fry for 30 seconds, then add the lemon rind and prawns and toss over the heat for 1 minute only. Remove from the heat and add the lemon juice.

Divide the mixture between 4 ramekins or similar moulds and press with the back of a spoon. Refrigerate for at least 1 hour, preferably longer. In a bowl, thoroughly mix the garam masala with the cream. Chill in the refrigerator.

Fifteen minutes before serving, place the asparagus in a large pan in a single layer. Add sufficient slightly salted boiling water to just cover and cook for about 12-15 minutes, until tender.

Meanwhile unmould the pressed prawns by dipping the base of each ramekin into boiling water for a few seconds, then if necessary slide a knife around the inside of each dish. Invert the pressed prawns on to individual plates. Drain the asparagus, arrange 3 spears on each plate and serve.

PIQUANT CHICKEN WITH CORIANDER AND LIME SAUCES

finely grated rind and juice of 2 limes
2 cloves garlic, crushed
50 g (2 oz) unsalted butter
10 ml (2 tsp) ground coriander
4 chicken breast fillets
salt and freshly ground black pepper

Coriander Sauce:
125 ml (4 fl oz) full-cream milk
225 g (8 oz) block creamed coconut
225 g (8 oz) fresh coriander leaves, finely
* chopped*
125 ml (4 fl oz) double cream

Lime Sauce:
finely grated rind and juice of 6 limes
5 ml (1 tsp) light soft brown sugar

Mix the lime rind and juice with the garlic, butter and coriander; set aside. Remove any sinews from the chicken. Lay out each chicken breast flat, cover with greaseproof paper and beat lightly to flatten, ensuring that the flesh is not broken. Spread both sides of each chicken breast with the flavoured butter, then roll up and wrap tightly in foil, so that none of the juices may escape. Chill in the refrigerator for 30 minutes, then cook in a preheated oven at 190°C (375° F) mark 5 for 40 minutes.

Meanwhile prepare the sauces. For the coriander sauce, place the milk and creamed coconut in a saucepan and heat gently, stirring, until all of the coconut is dissolved. Add the coriander and cook very gently, stirring frequently, for 10 minutes. Purée the sauce in a blender or food processor, then stir in the cream and heat through gently.

For the lime sauce, heat the lime juice and grated rind with the sugar. Unwrap the chicken and add the pan juices to the lime sauce. Reduce to a glaze.

Place the chicken on individual plates, spoon over the lime sauce to glaze and serve with the coriander sauce, spiced rice and glazed French beans.

SPICED BROWN AND WILD RICE

1.2 litres (2 pints) light chicken stock
50 g (2 oz) wild rice
1.25 ml (¼ tsp) salt
12 green cardamom pods
25 g (1 oz) unsalted butter
225 g (8 oz) basmati brown rice

Bring the stock to the boil in a saucepan. Add the wild rice and salt, cover and cook for 10 minutes.

Meanwhile, extract the seeds from the cardamom pods and crush them with a pestle and mortar. Heat the butter in a pan, add the crushed cardamom seeds with the brown rice and fry gently for 5 minutes.

Add the brown rice mixture to the wild rice and stock, stir once only, cover and simmer for 35 minutes until tender.

To serve, press the rice mixture in individual moulds, then turn out on to individual plates. Serve immediately.

GLAZED FRENCH BEANS

225 g (8 oz) French beans, trimmed
15 ml (1 tbsp) light brown sugar

Cut the French beans into 2.5 cm (1 inch) lengths. Place in a wide pan, just cover with boiling water and add the sugar. Cook for 5 minutes until tender and glazed. If any liquid remains, boil rapidly to reduce. Serve the glazed beans in neat bundles.

Vegetable, Fruit and Nut Samosas with accompaniments
NICHOLAS POUND'S MAIN COURSE (REGIONAL HEAT)

Iced Coffee Amaretti Soufflés
SARAH MARSH'S DESSERT (REGIONAL HEAT)

WHITE CHOCOLATE ICE CREAM ON A DARK CHOCOLATE AND HAZELNUT BASE WITH A RASPBERRY SAUCE

Ice Cream:
225 g (8 oz) white chocolate
90 ml (3 fl oz) double cream
45 ml (3 tbsp) Drambuie
2 eggs, size 2, at room temperature,
    separated

Hazelnut Base:
175 g (6 oz) dark chocolate
110 g (4 oz) shelled hazelnuts
60 ml (2 fl oz) double cream

Sauce:
450 g (1 lb) raspberries

To Decorate:
mint or dill sprigs

Melt the white chocolate in a bowl over a pan of hot but not boiling water; watch carefully as this easily re-solidifies in a rather unpleasant way! Remove from the heat and add the cream and liqueur. Allow to cool for 5 minutes, then stir in the egg yolks. Whisk the egg whites until stiff, then gradually fold into the cooled mixture, using a metal spoon. Divide between 4 ramekins and place in the freezer for 2 hours on fast-freeze; 4 hours at standard freezer temperature.

To make the hazelnut base, melt the dark chocolate in a bowl over a pan of hot water. Meanwhile toast the hazelnuts under a preheated grill, turning frequently, until evenly browned. Chop them roughly and leave to cool. Add the cream to the melted chocolate, stir thoroughly, then add the hazelnuts. Divide the mixture between 4 individual flan tins, a little wider than the ramekins used for the ice cream. Chill in the refrigerator until firm.

Press the raspberries through a sieve into a jug, then chill in the refrigerator until required.

To serve, remove the hazelnut bases from their tins and place on individual serving plates. Have ready a bowl containing 1 cm (½ inch) depth of hot water. Dip the base of each ramekin into the hot water for a few seconds only, then turn out on to the hazelnut bases.

Surround with raspberry sauce and serve, decorated with mint or dill.

Regional Heats
The South East
Sarah Giles • Sarah Marsh • Caroline Mugford

— Winner —

Sarah Giles' Menu

Starter

Warm Goat's Cheese Salad with a Walnut Dressing

"Good classic combination. I don't need to say anything, I will have some more" Paul Rankin

"Qualities of simplicity and real flavour. Brilliant marriage" Loyd

Main Course

Medallions of Venison with Blackberry Sauce
Rösti Potatoes
Carrots and Kohlrabi in Honey and Ginger

Dessert

Pear and Calvados Sorbet in Chocolate Baskets

"A real refreshing burst" Paul Rankin

Sarah lives in Kent and is a sub editor on 'Living' magazine, which she joined from 'Country Homes and Interiors'. She writes features on various subjects for the magazine. Sarah owns a pony and loves riding. She also enjoys taking photographs, especially of sporting events. Somehow she still finds time to give dinner parties.

WARM GOAT'S CHEESE SALAD WITH A WALNUT DRESSING

selection of salad leaves, eg frisée, radicchio, lamb's lettuce
2 Somerset Goat's cheeses

Dressing:
5 ml (1 tsp) light soft brown sugar
5 ml (1 tsp) Dijon mustard
1.25 ml (¼ tsp) salt
2.5 ml (½ tsp) freshly ground black pepper
135 ml (4½ fl oz) walnut oil
30 ml (2 tbsp) cider vinegar
15 ml (1 tbsp) shelled walnuts, finely chopped
15 ml (1 tbsp) chopped sage leaves

Arrange the salad leaves on individual plates. To make the dressing, in a bowl whisk together the sugar, mustard, salt, pepper and walnut oil until well blended. Add the cider vinegar and whisk again. Cover and leave in the refrigerator until required.

Meanwhile, cut each cheese in half horizontally and grill under a fairly high heat, cut side up, until melting and just golden. Arrange on the salad leaves. Add the walnuts and sage to the dressing at the last minute and drizzle over the salad to serve.

MEDALLIONS OF VENISON WITH BLACKBERRY SAUCE

225 g (8 oz) blackberries
60 ml (4 tbsp) eau-de-vie de mure (berry brandy)
500 ml (16 fl oz) chicken or vegetable stock
90 ml (3 fl oz) ruby port
few drops of lemon juice, to taste
salt and freshly ground pepper
knob of butter
4 medallions of venison fillet
blackberry leaves to garnish (optional)

Set aside 8 blackberries, for garnish; press the rest of the blackberries through a sieve into a bowl and stir in the brandy.

Pour the stock and port into a saucepan and bring to the boil. Continue boiling until slightly reduced. Add the blackberries and brandy and continue to reduce until the sauce is thick enough to coat the back of a spoon. Check the seasoning and add lemon juice to taste.

Melt the butter in a shallow frying pan and fry the venison medallions for 6 minutes until tender, turning once. Pour a little sauce on to each serving plate and position a medallion on top. Garnish with the reserved blackberries and leaves if using. Serve immediately, with rösti potatoes, and carrots and kohlrabi in honey and ginger.

Rösti Potatoes

4 medium potatoes
½ large onion, finely chopped
25 g (1 oz) butter

Parboil the potatoes in boiling salted water for 10 minutes. When cool enough to handle, grate coarsely and mix with the onion. Melt the butter and lightly grease 8 deep patty tins. Fill with spoonfuls of the potato mixture and pour a little melted butter over each one. Bake in a preheated oven at 200°C (400°F) mark 6 for 15 minutes. Serve immediately.

Carrots and Kohlrabi in Honey and Ginger

6 baby carrots
2 small kohlrabi
salt
grated rind and juice of ½ lemon
15 ml (1 tbsp) honey
2 cm (¾ inch) piece fresh root ginger, grated
1 green pepper

Cut the carrots and kohlrabi into julienne strips and cook in approximately 150 ml (¼ pint) boiling salted water with the lemon rind and juice, honey and ginger added, until tender.

Cut four rings from the pepper and use to secure bundles of carrot and kohlrabi julienne, to serve.

PEAR AND CALVADOS SORBET IN CHOCOLATE BASKETS

Pear Sorbet:
4 ripe pears
20 ml (1½ tbsp) white wine
100 g (4 oz) sugar
300 ml (½ pint) water
juice of 2 lemons
grated rind of 1 lemon
15 ml (1 tbsp) Calvados

Chocolate Baskets:
25 g (1 oz) butter
25 g (1 oz) caster sugar
15 ml (1 tbsp) golden syrup
25 g (1 oz) plain flour
2.5 ml (½ tsp) ground ginger
2.5 ml (½ tsp) brandy
grated rind of ¼ lemon
100 g (4 oz) plain chocolate
20 ml (1½ tbsp) milk
15 ml (1 tbsp) rum

To Decorate:
lime rind twists

First make the sorbet. Halve, peel and core the pears and roughly chop them. Place in a saucepan with the wine and cook until soft and pulpy. Mash with a potato masher if necessary.

Dissolve the sugar in the water in a pan over low heat, then remove from the heat. Stir in the lemon juice and rind, with the Calvados, then add to the pears, stirring well. Leave to cool.

Transfer the pear mixture to an ice-cream maker and churn for about 20-25 minutes until just firm. Scoop into a freezerproof container and transfer to the freezer until required. Alternatively if you do not have an ice-cream maker, freeze the sorbet in a shallow freezer-proof container until semi-frozen, whisk to break down the ice crystals, then freeze until firm.

Meanwhile make the chocolate baskets. Melt the butter in a saucepan with the sugar and golden syrup. Sift the flour with the ginger and stir into the mixture, then add the brandy and lemon rind. Drop 4 heaped teaspoonfuls on a baking tray lined with non-stick baking parchment, spacing them well apart. Bake in a preheated oven at 180°C (350°F) mark 4 for about 8 minutes until golden and lacy. Remove from the oven and quickly mould each one over an upturned glass to shape into baskets. Carefully remove when set and transfer to a wire rack to cool and harden.

Melt the chocolate with the milk in a heatproof bowl over a pan of gently simmering water, then brush over the cooled baskets, inside and out. Leave to set.

Serve a scoop of sorbet in each chocolate basket and decorate with twists of lemon rind.

REGIONAL HEATS
The South East
Sarah Giles • Sarah Marsh • Caroline Mugford

Sarah Marsh's Menu

STARTER
Stuffed Trout in a Bacon Jacket with Horseradish Sauce

MAIN COURSE
Wild Rabbit in Cider and Rosemary
Prune-stuffed Baked Apples
Puréed Parsnips
Mangetout

DESSERT

Iced Coffee Amaretti Soufflés
"THAT IS YUMMY" LOYD

Sarah read medieval history at Exeter University, and has since established herself as an interior designer. She runs a successful business in Surrey with her mother painting antique furniture, chests, cupboards, bedheads, etc. Earlier this year she spent two months in India and is now writing a book from her extensive travel journals.

STUFFED TROUT IN A BACON JACKET WITH HORSERADISH SAUCE

25 g (1 oz) green pepper, cored and seeded
25 g (1 oz) red pepper, cored and seeded
50 g (2 oz) blue cheese
100 g (4 oz) goat's cheese
squeeze of lime juice
salt and freshly ground black pepper
9-10 very thin slices streaky bacon
1 medium trout, filleted and skin removed

Horseradish Sauce:
125 ml (4 fl oz) Greek-style natural yogurt
10-15 ml (2-3 tsp) grated fresh horseradish
5 ml (1 tsp) clear honey
5 ml (1 tsp) lime juice

To Garnish:
cucumber slices
lime slices
mint sprigs

Finely dice the peppers. Mash the cheeses together with the lime juice, then add the diced peppers and seasoning.

Lay the bacon slices side by side on a plate or small board. Place one trout fillet across the middle of the bacon and spread the cheese filling evenly over the fish. Cover this with the second trout fillet and wrap the bacon round the fish 'sandwich' to enclose it, trimming the ends of the bacon slices.

Lay a sheet of greaseproof paper over the fish and cover it with a baking sheet, then invert everything, so that the fish is lying on the baking sheet, with the bacon joins underneath.

Bake in a preheated oven at 180°C (350° F) mark 4 for 20-25 minutes. Baste with the cooking juices, then leave to cool. Chill before serving.

Mix together the ingredients for the horseradish sauce and season with salt and pepper to taste.

Cut the trout into slices, between the bacon pieces. Assemble two slices on each plate. Add a spoonful of horse-radish sauce and garnish with cucumber, lime slices and mint sprigs to serve.

WILD RABBIT IN CIDER AND ROSEMARY

4 rabbit joints
15 ml (1 tbsp) flour
15 ml (1 tbsp) English mustard powder
30 ml (2 tbsp) sunflower oil
30 ml (2 tbsp) olive oil
knob of butter
1 onion, chopped
150 ml (¼ pint) cider
300 ml (½ pint) rabbit stock
1 rosemary sprig
1 bay leaf
5 ml (1 tsp) brown sugar
salt and freshly ground black pepper
chopped parsley to garnish

If the joints are from an older rabbit, remove the sinews in the hind legs. Toss the rabbit joints in the flour and mustard powder (it is easiest to do this in a plastic bag). Reserve the excess flour mixture.

Heat the sunflower and olive oils in a flameproof casserole, add the rabbit joints and seal on all sides. Remove the rabbit and set aside. Add the butter to the casserole dish, add the onion and sweat until softened. Stir in the remaining flour and cook, stirring, for 1-2 minutes. Gradually stir in the cider, followed by the stock. Bring to the boil, adding the rosemary, bay leaf, seasoning and brown sugar. Return the rabbit joints to the casserole, cover and cook in a preheated oven at 160°C (325°F) mark 3 for 1¼-1½ hours.

Serve garnished with parsley and accompanied by prune-stuffed baked apples, puréed parsnips and mangetout.

PRUNE-STUFFED BAKED APPLES

These taste delicious if you soak the prunes in sufficient port to cover generously, with a few strips of pared orange rind added, for 1-2 days beforehand.

4 eating apples, preferably red ones
12-16 prunes (pitted), soaked in port
    flavoured with orange rind
2 cinnamon sticks
4 cloves
10 ml (2 tsp) soft brown sugar

Select a baking dish into which the apples fit snugly. Remove the cores from the apples, using an apple corer, then score the skin round the middle of each one to prevent it bursting during cooking. Drain the prunes, reserving the port; discard the orange rind. Stuff the apples with the prunes.

Put the apples into the baking dish and add the reserved port, cinnamon sticks, cloves, sugar and a little water if necessary. Cover the dish with foil and bake in a preheated oven at 160°C (325°F) mark 3 for 40-45 minutes until tender.

PURÉED PARSNIPS

350 g (12 oz) parsnips
150 ml (¼ pint) well-flavoured stock
  (preferably rabbit stock)
25 g (1 oz) butter
90-120 ml (3-5 fl oz) single cream
5 ml (1 tsp) caster sugar
5 ml (1 tsp) lemon juice
freshly grated nutmeg

Peel the parsnips and cut into even-sized pieces, removing any woody stems. Bring the rabbit stock to the boil in a saucepan. Add the parsnips and simmer for 10-15 minutes until tender, topping up with water as necessary. Drain and press through a sieve into a bowl lined with muslin. Let cool for a moment, then twist the muslin to squeeze out as much liquid as possible.

Melt the butter with 90 ml (3 fl oz) of the cream in a non-stick pan, then add the sugar, lemon juice and nutmeg to taste. Lower the heat and add the parsnip purée a spoonful at a time, stirring in well and adding more cream as necessary. Heat the purée through, and keep warm if necessary in a bain marie until ready to serve.

ICED COFFEE AMARETTI SOUFFLÉS

12 amaretti biscuits
2 egg whites
175 g (6 oz) vanilla sugar (see note)
90 ml (6 tbsp) water
7.5 ml (1½ tsp) instant coffee dissolved in
  7.5 ml (1½ tsp) hot water, or very strong
  black coffee
15 ml (1 tbsp) Grand Marnier
350 ml (12 fl oz) double cream

To Serve:
4 toasted whole almonds
icing sugar for dusting

Prepare 4 ramekins by securing a non-stick baking parchment collar around each one, to stand 5 cm (2 inches) above the rims. Put the amaretti biscuits in a plastic bag and crush with a rolling pin.

Whisk the egg whites until stiff. Dissolve the sugar in the water in a heavy-based saucepan over a gentle heat, then bring to the boil and bubble for 3 minutes. Pour the syrup onto the egg whites in a thin stream, whisking constantly at a high speed. Continue whisking until cool, then add the coffee and Grand Marnier. Whip the cream in a separate bowl until thick but not stiff, then lightly fold into the mixture.

Spoon the soufflé mixture into the ramekins until they are just over half-full, then sprinkle on a thick layer of crushed biscuits Cover with the remaining soufflé mixture, until it stands 2.5 cm (1 inch) above the rims.

Freeze the soufflés for 1½-2 hours, then carefully remove the paper collars. Coat the sides and tops with the remaining crushed biscuits and place a toasted almond on the top of each one. Dust the tops with sifted icing sugar.

Note: Leave a vanilla pod in a jar of caster sugar to impart flavour.

THE SOUTH EAST

SARAH GILES • SARAH MARSH • CAROLINE MUGFORD

CAROLINE MUGFORD'S MENU

STARTER
Aromatic Steamed Scallops on a bed of Tagliatelli with a Tarragon Jus

MAIN COURSE
Smoked Ballotine of Two Fish with Cream of Leek Sauce Caramelised Vegetables - Parsnip, Celeriac and Carrots

DESSERT
Chilled Apple and Lemon Soufflé with Apple and Calvados Coulis

"CAN I MAKE IT TO THE NEXT TABLE, IT WAS REALLY DELICIOUS"

VIRGINIA LENG

Caroline is a Production Manager for a London design company. She is married and lives in an enchanting cottage with its own clock-tower in picturesque Liphook. Caroline still maintains a talent for painting from her art college background and is often commissioned to paint portraits.

AROMATIC STEAMED SCALLOPS ON A BED OF TAGLIATELLE WITH A TARRAGON JUS

450 g (1 lb) queen scallops (about 5 per person), cleaned
handful of tarragon sprigs
few rosemary sprigs
sprinkling of cumin seeds
strip of lemon rind

Tagliatelle:
275 g (9 oz) plain white flour
2 eggs, plus 1 egg yolk
pinch of salt
60 ml (4 tbsp) water
15 ml (1 tbsp) chlorophyll of spinach (see below)

Jus:
300 ml (½ pint) light fish stock
few tarragon sprigs, chopped
a little chopped rosemary (optional)
15 ml (1 tbsp) lemon juice

To make the pasta, put all the ingredients – in the above order – into a food processor and work for about 30 seconds until evenly blended. Knead until smooth, then wrap and leave to rest in the refrigerator for 1 hour. Pass through a pasta machine to the desired thickness and width. Alternatively roll out very thinly and cut into strips.

To prepare the jus, place the fish stock in a saucepan with the herbs and fast boil until reduced to a very light syrup, about 5 minutes. Sharpen with lemon juice.

For the scallops, line a bamboo steamer or similar container with muslin to hold the herbs. Arrange a bed of herbs on the muslin. Add the cumin seeds and lemon, then place the scallops on top. Steam over a pan of boiling water for approximately 5 minutes, depending on size, until just cooked; do not overcook.

Cook the tagliatelle in plenty of boiling salted water until al dente (just tender), about 2 minutes. Drain thoroughly.

Serve the scallops on a bed of tagliatelle and spoon the jus around them.

Chlorophyll of spinach: To prepare this use 250 g (9 oz) fresh spinach and 550 ml (18 fl oz) water. Discard the stalks from the spinach, thoroughly rinse the leaves, then purée in a blender or food processor with the water. Strain through a fine sieve, then through a muslin-lined sieve into a small pan. Slowly bring to the boil. The rising temperature will bring the chlorophyll to the surface, which can then be scooped off with a spoon. You should obtain about 45 ml (3 tbsp) from this quantity.

Smoked Ballotine of Two Fish with Cream of Leek Sauce

Ballotine:
*250 g (9 oz) middle cut fillet of salmon,
   skinned*
9 medium spinach leaves
1 egg white
salt and freshly ground black pepper
75 g (3 oz) unsalted butter, softened
175 g (6 oz) lemon sole, skinned
225 ml (7½ fl oz) whipping cream
225 ml (7½ fl oz) double cream
3 drops of hickory smoke (optional)
*3 cooked slices smoked back bacon, cut
   into strips (optional)*

Leek Sauce:
400 g (14 oz) leeks
100 g (4 oz) butter
450 ml (¾ pint) double cream
1.25 ml (¼ tsp) salt
plenty of freshly ground black pepper

Cut two horizontal slices from the salmon fillet, each about 3 mm (⅛ inch) thick. Lay side by side on a large sheet of greaseproof paper, cover with another sheet of greaseproof paper and flatten to approximately 10 x 15 cm (4 x 6 inches). Chill in the refrigerator.

Meanwhile blanch the spinach leaves in boiling water for 20 seconds, refresh in cold water and drain.

Put the remaining salmon in a food processor or blender with half the egg white and salt and work to a purée, adding 40 g (1½ oz) butter, while the machine is running. Transfer to a bowl. Purée the sole with the remaining egg white, salt and remaining butter in the same way. Rest the fish purées in the refrigerator for about 15 minutes.

Stir the creams together. Return the salmon purée to the food processor or blender and gradually add half of the cream mixture through the feeder tube

very slowly as the friction of the blades and the fat content may cause the mousse to separate. Add half of the hickory smoke flavouring at this stage if using. Repeat with the sole mousse, remaining cream and flavouring (if using). Leave the fish mousses to rest in the refrigerator for about 15 minutes.

Season the salmon fillets and cover with a thin layer of sole mousse. Add a layer of spinach leaves, then cover with another thin layer of sole mousse. At this stage you can add the bacon strips, if required, in a line down the middle .

Roll the fillet up like a Swiss roll, taking care not to handle it too much, and wrap tightly in greaseproof paper. Chill in the refrigerator. On a separate sheet of greaseproof paper, spread half of the salmon mousse and make a groove down the centre to accommodate the rolled fillet. Cover with remaining salmon mousse and shape into a cylinder. Wrap the ballotine in a double thickness of muslin and secure tightly. Tie loosely with string at 3 equally spaced places to ensure even cooking. (The string should not be too tight as the mousse expands on cooking.)

Poach in salted and barely simmering water covered with a heavy cloth to keep the roll immersed for 35-40 minutes. Test after 35 minutes, inserting a long needle into the centre; the mousse is cooked if the needle feels lukewarm.

Meanwhile prepare the sauce. Finely slice the leeks into 3 mm (⅛ inch) rounds. Melt the butter in a saucepan and sauté the leeks for 5 minutes. Add the cream, salt and plenty of pepper and reduce over a medium heat to the required thickness (and strength of flavour). If a smooth sauce is preferred, purée in a food processor or blender, then pass through a fine sieve.

Unwrap the ballotine and cut into slices. Serve with the leek sauce.

CARAMELISED VEGETABLES

250 g (9 oz) celeriac
250 g (9 oz) parsnip
225 g (8 oz) carrots
225 g (8 oz) butter
30 ml (2 tbsp) white wine vinegar
30 ml (2 tbsp) demerara sugar
freshly ground black pepper

Cut the vegetables into equal-sized pieces, no thicker than 5 mm (¼ inch). Melt the butter in a saucepan over a medium heat, add the celeriac and cook for 5 minutes. Add the parsnip and cook for a further 15-20 minutes. Add the carrots with the wine vinegar and sugar and boil rapidly for a few minutes to allow the juices to reduce slightly. Keep testing the vegetables during cooking; their size will determine the cooking time. Season with pepper to serve.

CHILLED APPLE AND LEMON SOUFFLÉ WITH APPLE AND CALVADOS COULIS

2½ leaves gelatine
275 ml (9 fl oz) milk
900 ml (1½ pints) double cream
1 vanilla pod
6 egg yolks
100 g (3½ oz) caster sugar
25 g (1 oz) plain flour
20 g (¾ oz) cornflour
6-8 Cox's apples
30 ml (2 tbsp) demerara sugar
grated rind and juice of 2 lemons
freshly grated nutmeg to taste
ground cinnamon to taste
60 ml (2 fl oz) Calvados (apple brandy)

Prepare 4 ramekins by securing a greaseproof paper collar around each one so that it stands about 4 cm (1½ inches) above the rim. Soak the gelatine leaves in cold water to cover for 15 minutes to soften.

Put the milk and 300 ml (½ pint) cream in a saucepan with the vanilla pod, bring to the boil and allow to simmer for a few minutes. Meanwhile in a bowl, whisk together the egg yolks and sugar, then mix in the flour and cornflour until smooth. Gradually whisk in one third of the milk, then add to the rest of the milk in the pan. Cook gently for about 2 minutes whisking constantly until a smooth custard is formed; do not allow to boil or it will curdle. Strain into a bowl.

Meanwhile peel, core and chop the apples and place in a saucepan with the sugar, lemon rind and juice, and spices. Cover and cook until soft. Purée the apples and pass through a sieve. Set aside 30 ml (2 tbsp) apple purée for the sauce.

Squeeze the gelatine leaves to remove excess liquid, then add to the warm custard with the hot apple purée and stir until dissolved. Leave to cool.

Whip the rest of the cream until it is thick enough to leave a ribbon when the whisk is lifted, then carefully fold into the apple custard. Divide equally between the prepared ramekins and chill in the refrigerator for 2-3 hours until set.

Heat the reserved apple purée with the Calvados and reduce slightly, then leave to cool.

Just before serving, remove the paper collars. Spoon out a little of the mixture from the centre of each soufflé and add a little of the apple and Calvados coulis. Replace the soufflé mixture. Serve accompanied by the rest of the coulis.

REGIONAL HEATS

SCOTLAND & NORTHERN IRELAND

MARTHA SPENCER • CARYL DOHERTY • SCOTT FINDLAY

WINNER

MARTHA SPENCER'S MENU

STARTER

*Arbroath Smokie Mousse with Shredded Vegetables
and Vinaigrette*

MAIN COURSE

Spiced Venison Fillet

Mashed Potatoes

Caramelised Shallots

"SOMETHING YOU WANT TO COME HOME TO AFTER TRAMPING OVER
THE MOORS" LOYD

DESSERT

Warm Baked Lemon Tart

Like Loyd Grossman, Martha comes from Boston, where she worked for a financial company. She is presently living in Angus, Scotland, with her husband and dog, in Airlie Castle which they have leased for a number of years. Martha enjoys dressmaking and making patchwork quilts, which are hung around the castle. Painting is another passion and she uses a cottage attached to the castle as her studio.

ARBROATH SMOKIE MOUSSE WITH SHREDDED VEGETABLES AND VINAIGRETTE

If you are filleting the fish yourself, first warm it slightly in the oven as this enables the flesh to be removed more easily.

1 large Arbroath smokie, skinned and
*   filleted, 300 g (10 oz) filleted weight*
2 eggs
salt and freshly ground black pepper
200 ml (7 fl oz) double or soured cream

Shredded Vegetables:
1 carrot
1 courgette
1 small cooked beetroot

Vinaigrette:
7.5 ml (1½ tsp) Dijon mustard
22 ml (1½ tbsp) oil (preferably white
*   truffle oil)*
7.5 ml (1½ tsp) white wine vinegar

Base:
100 g (4 oz) cabbage, finely shredded
25 g (1 oz) butter
25 g (1 oz) pine nuts, toasted

Purée the fish in a blender or food processor with the eggs and salt and pepper. Transfer to a bowl, cover and chill in the refrigerator for 1 hour.

Butter 4 individual moulds, each about 120 ml (4 fl oz) capacity. Line a bain-marie (or roasting tin) with greaseproof paper.

Gradually incorporate the cream into the fish mixture, then pass the mixture through a food mill to remove any bones. Spoon the smokie mixture into the moulds and place in the bain-marie; the hot water should come halfway up the sides of the moulds. Cover with a sheet of foil that has been pierced in a few places. Cook in a preheated oven at 160°C (325°F) mark 3 for about 20-30 minutes until set.

Meanwhile, finely grate the carrot, courgette and beetroot, keeping them separate. Combine the ingredients for the vinaigrette and season with salt and pepper to taste.

Just before serving, sauté the cabbage in the butter until crisp and tender. Add the pine nuts; do not overcook cabbage.

To serve, place a little of the cabbage in the centre of each warmed serving plate and unmould the mousses on top of the cabbage. Decorate with the shredded vegetables, arranging them one on top of another. Warm the vinaigrette and pour around the vegetables to serve.

SPICED VENISON FILLET

It's essential to use a good quality homemade stock for this dish.

2 venison fillet steaks, total weight about
*   700 g (1½ lb)*
900 ml (1½ pints) venison stock
15 ml (1 tbsp) coriander seeds
15 ml (1 tbsp) cumin seeds
15 ml (1 tbsp) black peppercorns
about 200 g (7 oz) clarified butter

To Garnish:
16-20 slices unsmoked back bacon

Bring the stock to the boil and simmer until reduced by about two-thirds to a coating consistency. Set this sauce aside.

Toast all of the spices and grind them together in an electric grinder until very fine. Roll the venison fillets in the ground spices, pressing them firmly into the meat. Cut the venison fillets into 2.5 cm (1 inch) medallions.

Heat at least 5 mm (¼ inch) depth of clarified butter in a heavy-based pan until very hot, then add the venison fillets and sauté until they are dark brown and crusty on the outside, but still quite rare inside. Meanwhile fry the bacon until crispy.

Serve the venison fillets on warmed plates with a large scoop of mashed potato and the caramelised shallots. Garnish with the bacon slices and add a ladleful of sauce. Serve the remaining sauce separately.

MASHED POTATOES

400 g (14 oz) potatoes, peeled
100 g (4 oz) butter
100 ml (3½ fl oz) hot milk
salt and freshly ground black pepper

Cook the potatoes in boiling salted water until tender. Drain thoroughly, then push the potatoes through a food mill to mash smoothly. Stir the butter and the milk through the mashed potato to give a smooth creamy mix. Season with salt and pepper and serve hot, with the spiced venison.

CARAMELISED SHALLOTS

20 shallots, peeled
15 ml (1 tbsp) butter
15 ml (1 tbsp) oil
250 ml (8 fl oz) beef stock

Brown the shallots in the butter and oil in a pan over moderate heat, turning frequently. Add the stock and bring to the boil. Lower the heat, cover and simmer for about 15-20 minutes until the shallots are tender.

Steamed Guinea Fowl with Ravioli of Wild Mushrooms
SCOTT FINDLAY'S MAIN COURSE (REGIONAL HEAT)

Pheasant Pie with Potato Pastry
LINDA YEWDALL'S MAIN COURSE (SEMI-FINAL)

WARM BAKED LEMON TART

Pâte Sablée:
250 g (9 oz) flour
200 g (7 oz) butter, diced
100 g (3½ oz) icing sugar, sifted
pinch of salt
1 egg, size 3
1 vanilla pod, split
finely grated rind of 1 lemon
beaten egg, to glaze

Filling:
2 lemons
5 eggs
200 g (7 oz) caster sugar
185 ml (6 fl oz) double cream
50 g (2 oz) icing sugar

To Serve:
double cream

To make the pâte sablée, sift the flour into a mixing bowl and make a well in the centre. Add the diced butter to the well, then gradually work it with your fingertips until very soft. Sift the icing sugar on to the butter, add the salt and work into the butter. Add the egg and mix well. Gradually draw in the flour with your fingertips and mix until completely amalgamated. Add the seeds from the vanilla pod and the grated lemon rind and work into the dough. Wrap and chill in the refrigerator for 1 hour.

Grease a 20 cm (8 inch) flan ring with butter and place in the freezer for 10 minutes. Roll out the pastry on a lightly floured surface to a thickness of 5 mm (¼ inch). Place the prepared flan ring on a baking sheet and line with the pastry. Leave to rest in the refrigerator for 15 minutes.

For the filling, wash the lemons thoroughly, then finely grate the zests. Squeeze the juice, then strain. In a bowl, lightly beat the eggs and sugar with a whisk until smooth and well blended. Lightly whisk the cream in another bowl for about 10 seconds, until slightly thickened. Stir the lemon zests and juice into the beaten eggs, then whisk in the cream. Cover and chill in the refrigerator.

Line the pastry case with foil and fill with baking beans. Bake in a preheated oven at 200°C (400°F) mark 6 for 15 minutes, then remove the beans and foil. Brush the inside with beaten egg and return to the oven for about 5 minutes, until the glaze is lightly coloured.

Lower the oven temperature to 150°C (300°F) mark 2. Lightly stir the filling and pour into the pastry case; bake at once for about 1 hour.

Trim the edges of the cooked pastry with a small knife, so that the rim of the tart stands 5 mm (¼ inch) above the filling. Slide a knife between the flan ring and the tart and gently lift off. Sprinkle the top with icing sugar and caramelise with a blow torch if you like! Serve warm, with double cream.

Note: This lemon tart will serve 6-8 people. It is also delicious served cold, but do not store it in the refrigerator or the pastry will become soggy.

REGIONAL HEATS
SCOTLAND & NORTHERN IRELAND
MARTHA SPENCER • CARYL DOHERTY • SCOTT FINDLAY

CARYL DOHERTY'S MENU

STARTER
Salmon and Avocado with Sun-dried Tomato Vinaigrette

MAIN COURSE
Fillet of Beef with Juniper and Thyme Sauce
Carrot Mousse
Roasted Parsnips
Broccoli Florets

DESSERT
Mille Feuilles of Caramelised Apples with Toffee Sauce
"THAT IS A GREAT PUDDING" LOYD

Caryl is married to a solicitor and has two children aged, 6 years and 4 years, who occupy most of her time. They live in a delightful period house with an attractive garden which Caryl spends a lot of time looking after. One of her main obsessions is picking up bargains at local auctions.

SALMON AND AVOCADO WITH SUN-DRIED TOMATO VINAIGRETTE

4 ripe avocados
4 salmon fillets, each weighing 100 g (4 oz)
salt and freshly ground black pepper

Dressing:
100 ml (3½ fl oz) light olive oil
20 ml (4 tsp) wine vinegar
7.5 ml (½ tbsp) Dijon mustard
25 g (1 oz) sun-dried tomatoes

Put the ingredients for the dressing in a food processor or blender with salt and pepper to taste and work until smooth.

Halve and stone the avocados, then cut in half again lengthwise and peel. Cut each quarter evenly into 4 slices and arrange on individual plates.

Season the salmon with salt and pepper to taste and cook under a preheated grill for 3 to 4 minutes maximum, turning once. Arrange on the serving plates with the avocados and surround with the dressing. Serve immediately.

CARROT MOUSSE

350 g (12 oz) carrots
25 g (1 oz) butter
2 strips of orange rind
200 ml (7 fl oz) strong chicken stock
2 eggs
pinch of ground mace
pinch of freshly grated nutmeg
salt and freshly ground black pepper

Peel the carrots, cut in half, discard the central core and dice. Melt the butter in a pan over gentle heat and add the orange rind. Sweat the carrots in the butter until they lose their hardness, about 10 minutes. Add the stock and cook until completely absorbed. Discard the orange rind.

Transfer the carrots to a blender or food processor, add the eggs and blend until smooth. Add the mace, nutmeg, salt and pepper to taste. Fill 4 buttered ramekins with the carrot purée. Place in a bain-marie or roasting tin containing enough hot water to come halfway up the sides of the ramekins. Cook in a preheated oven at 170°C (325°F) mark 3 for 25 minutes.

Turn out of the ramekins to serve.

FILLET OF BEEF WITH JUNIPER AND THYME SAUCE

Make sure you use well-hung beef for this dish.

700 g (1½ lb) fillet of beef, in one piece
¼ bottle of Madeira
¼ bottle of red wine
small bunch of herbs, ie thyme, parsley, chives, finely chopped
salt and freshly ground black pepper

Sauce:
beef bones
1 carrot, finely chopped
1 onion, finely chopped
1 celery stalk, finely chopped
25 g (1 oz) thyme leaves, chopped
12 juniper berries, crushed

First prepare the sauce. Place the beef bones in a roasting tin and cook in a preheated oven at 190°C (375°F) mark 5 for 30 minutes to brown; reserve the cooking juices. Transfer the bones to a large stock pot or heavy-based pan and add the carrot, onion, celery, thyme and juniper berries. Add sufficient water to cover, bring to the boil and reduce to 300 ml (½ pint) liquid, then strain through a sieve.

Place the reserved meat juices from the roasting tin in a clean saucepan and cook over a moderate heat for 3-4 minutes. Add the stock a little at a time, because you may only require 150 ml (¼ pint), and season with salt and pepper. Reduce to a coating thickness and pass through a sieve again. Heat through before serving.

Place the beef fillet in a shallow roasting tin with the Madeira and red wine. Roast in the preheated oven at 190°C (375°F) mark 5 for 15 minutes per 500 g (1 lb) for rare, or 20-25 minutes per 500 g (1 lb) for medium, basting occasionally with the juices. Turn off the oven, open the door and leave to rest for approximately 30 minutes.

After resting, roll the beef fillet in finely chopped herbs. Carve into slices and serve with the juniper and thyme sauce, carrot mousse, roasted parsnips and broccoli florets.

MILLE FEUILLES OF CARAMELISED APPLES WITH TOFFEE SAUCE

330 g (12 oz) sugar
60 g (2 oz) unsalted butter
3 sheets filo pastry
250 ml (8 fl oz) double cream
8 small Cox's apples
juice of ½ lemon

To Decorate:
8 apple slices
4 mint sprigs
icing sugar for dusting

Put 30 g (1 oz) sugar, 30 g (1 oz) butter and 30 ml (2 tbsp) water in a small saucepan over low heat until melted. Remove from the heat and cool slightly.

Place a sheet of filo pastry on a cold work surface and brush liberally with the cooled butter mix. When completely coated, place another sheet of filo on top and repeat the process. Cover with the third filo sheet and brush again. Cut out twelve 10 cm (4 inch) circles and place on greased baking trays. Bake in a preheated oven at 190°C (375°F) mark 5 for 5-6 minutes until cooked. Transfer to a wire rack to cool.

To make the toffee sauce put 100 g (4 oz) sugar in a small heavy-based saucepan with enough water to cover and heat gently until dissolved, then boil steadily until it reaches a light caramel stage. Remove from the heat and whisk in the cream. Set aside.

In another heavy-based saucepan, place 200 g (7 oz) sugar with enough water to cover. Heat gently until dissolved then cook to a darker caramel stage. Immediately remove from heat and add remaining butter, a little at a time, whisking gently to emulsify.

Peel, core and thickly slice the apples lengthwise and toss in the lemon juice. Place them in a shallow baking tin and cover with the butter caramel. Cook in a preheated oven at 200°C (400°F) mark 6 for about 15 minutes until the apples have caramelised, but remain firm.

Place a filo pastry disc on each serving plate and put one spoonful of apple mixture on top. Place another filo disc on top of this and cover with another spoonful of apples. Top with the final disc of filo pastry. Slowly heat the toffee sauce and drizzle round the base of each mille feuille. Decorate with apple slices and mint. Dust with a little icing sugar and serve immediately.

REGIONAL HEATS

SCOTLAND & NORTHERN IRELAND

MARTHA SPENCER • CARYL DOHERTY • SCOTT FINDLAY

SCOTT FINDLAY'S MENU

STARTER

Warm Smoked Salmon with Beurre Blanc

MAIN COURSE

Steamed Guinea Fowl with Ravioli of Wild
Mushrooms and Thyme Jus

"THAT IS DELICIOUS, GOSH IT IS!" CLAIRE MACDONALD

DESSERT

Tarte Tatin of Pears

"OH, MARVELLOUS, THAT IS QUITE SPECTACULAR" TREVOR MCDONALD

Scott lives in Edinburgh and runs a PR business with his wife, whom he met when he was working in London. They have one son and two working labradors. In his spare time, Scott loves to go fishing and shooting at Loch Tay. He also likes to sail. On his trips to the South, he and his wife enjoy a game of golf. In general, Scott is quite an outdoor man.

WARM SMOKED SALMON WITH BEURRE BLANC

Use wild salmon if possible, as it is slightly more oily than the salmon you usually buy and therefore does not dry out as quickly during cooking. If you get your fishmonger to descale and fillet the wild salmon for you, remember to ask for the bones as you will need them for the stock. You will also need oak chippings for cooking.

4 fillets of wild salmon, each
    weighing 100 g (4 oz)
2 cinnamon sticks
15 ml (1 tbsp) apple tea leaves
1 clove garlic, sliced

Fish Stock:

225 g (8 oz) salmon bones
150 ml (¼ pint) water
30 ml (2 tbsp) white wine
5 ml (1 tsp) chopped carrot
5 ml (1 tsp) chopped onion
5 ml (1 tsp) chopped leek, white part only
¼ bay leaf

Beurre Blanc:

3 shallots, chopped
150 g (5 oz) cold butter, diced
30 ml (2 tbsp) white wine vinegar
60 ml (4 tbsp) dry white wine
30 ml (2 tbsp) fish stock
5 ml (1 tsp) double cream
salt and freshly ground white pepper
pinch of sugar
5 ml (1 tsp) lemon juice
5 ml (1 tsp) light soy sauce

To Finish:

4 courgettes
oil for deep-frying
1 large tomato, skinned, seeded and diced

For the fish stock use the centre bone from the salmon and chop it into 3 pieces. Place in a saucepan with the water and wine. Bring to the boil and skim. Add the remaining stock ingredients and simmer for 15 minutes. Strain and set aside.

To make the beurre blanc, cook the shallots gently in 5 ml (1 tsp) of the butter until softened. Add the vinegar and white wine and reduce by half. Add the fish stock and cream and simmer for 1 minute, adding pepper to taste. Add the rest of the butter, a little at a time, whisking constantly, until melted, then bring to simmering point and add the sugar, lemon juice, soy sauce and a pinch of salt. Set aside.

Scatter oak chippings on the base of a fish kettle or other suitable container and sprinkle on the cinnamon, apple tea and garlic. Stand a wire rack 5 cm (2 inches) above this base and place the salmon fillets, skin side down, on the rack. Cover with a tight-fitting lid and cook over high heat for 8-12 minutes. The skin should be charred while the flesh of the salmon is barely cooked.

Meanwhile, shred the courgettes lengthwise to resemble straw, discarding the core. Heat the oil in a deep-fryer and deep-fry the courgettes briefly until crisp.

To serve, place the salmon fillets on warmed plates, skin side up and top with bundles of courgette 'straw'. Warm the butter sauce and spoon around the salmon. Sprinkle with the diced tomato and serve immediately.

STEAMED GUINEA FOWL WITH RAVIOLI OF WILD MUSHROOMS AND THYME JUS

4 guinea fowl chicks
8 thyme sprigs
salt and freshly ground white pepper
4 fresh or dried juniper berries
20 ml (4 tsp) each brandy, port and Madeira

Sauce:
50 g (2 oz) clarified butter
30 ml (2 tbsp) diced shallot
15 ml (1 tbsp) diced carrot
15 ml (1 tbsp) diced celery
3 cloves garlic, split
5 thyme sprigs
2.5 ml (½ tsp) white pepper
15 ml (1 tbsp) brandy
120 ml (4 fl oz) dry white wine
600 ml (1 pint) veal stock
150 ml (¼ pint) water
15 ml (1 tbsp) tomato purée
½ bay leaf
10 ml (2 tsp) cream

To Serve:
10 pencil-thin leeks, halved
8 shallots, chopped
225 g (8 oz) chanterelle mushrooms
225 g (8 oz) trumpet mushrooms
knob of butter
4 ravioli of wild mushrooms (see right)

Cut the backbone from the birds and reserve for stock. Cut off the wing tips and leg tips. Remove the wishbones and reserve. Place a sprig of thyme between the skin and breast of each bird. Season the bird cavities and add the juniper berries and 15 ml (1 tsp) each of brandy, port and Madeira. Place each bird in a roasting bag, expel the air and secure with a knot. Place in a pan of boiling water and steam for 20 minutes. Remove and leave to rest for 5 minutes.

Meanwhile, make the sauce. Heat the butter in a heavy-based pan and brown the guinea fowl bones. Add the shallot, carrot and celery, 1 split clove garlic, 1 thyme sprig and pepper. Cook for 2 minutes, then deglaze with the brandy. Cook for 2 minutes, then add the wine and reduce by half. Add the stock, water, tomato purée, bay leaf, 4 thyme sprigs and the remaining garlic. Bring to the boil, skim well and simmer for 10 minutes. Pass the sauce through a sieve lined with a double thickness of muslin. Return to the cleaned pan, bring back to the boil and reduce by half. Add the cream and seasoning. Whisk lightly and keep warm.

Blanch the leeks in boiling salted water for 1 minute; keep warm. Quickly sauté the shallots and mushrooms in a knob of butter to soften.

Remove the birds from the roasting bags. Carve off the breasts and legs and discard the skin. Remove the thigh bones. Arrange the guinea fowl breasts and legs on warmed serving plates. Arrange the ravioli, leeks and mushrooms around the meat. Spoon the sauce over the meat and ravioli to serve.

RAVIOLI OF WILD MUSHROOMS

Pasta Dough:
250 g (9 oz) strong plain flour (preferably Italian wheat flour type 00)
pinch of salt
few drops of olive oil
2 eggs, plus 3 yolks

Chicken Mousse:
75 g (3 oz) skinless chicken breast fillet, chopped
pinch of ground mace
5 ml (1 tsp) chopped tarragon
½ egg
5 ml (1 tsp) salt
125 ml (4 fl oz) double cream

Mushroom Filling:
4 shallots, finely chopped
225 g (8 oz) wild mushrooms, chopped
25 g (1 oz) butter
1 thyme sprig
½ clove garlic

To make the pasta dough, put the flour, salt and oil in a blender or food processor and mix for a few seconds. Add the eggs and extra yolks and knead for 1-2 minutes until smooth. Divide into 4 pieces, wrap and leave to rest in the refrigerator for 20 minutes. You will only need one portion, so freeze the rest for later use.

To make the chicken mousse, put the chicken, mace and tarragon in a blender or food processor and process for 1 minute. Add the egg and salt, then process for a further minute. Transfer to a bowl, cover and chill in the refrigerator for 15 minutes. Gradually stir in the cream, then press the mixture through a sieve. Chill until required.

For the mushroom filling, sauté the shallots and mushrooms in the butter, with the thyme and garlic, until soft. Drain thoroughly and dry in a cloth. Discard the thyme and garlic. Chill until required.

Cut the portion of pasta into 4 slices and sprinkle lightly with flour, then put each piece through a pasta machine on the first setting. Repeat on the third setting, then roll out on the fifth setting, taking care to avoid breaking the thin sheets. Flour the pasta during rolling if necessary. If you do not have a pasta machine, roll out as thinly as possible. Cut two 7.5 cm (3 inch) circles from each sheet of pasta.

Blend 30 ml (2 tbsp) of the chicken mousse with 30 ml (2 tbsp) mushroom mixture. Place 15 ml (1 tbsp) of this filling in the centre of each of 4 pasta circles. Moisten the pasta rim and top with the remaining pasta circles. Pinch the edges together to seal.

Poach the ravioli in plenty of salted boiling salted water for 2 minutes until al dente (just tender). Drain thoroughly and serve with the guinea fowl.

TARTE TATIN OF PEARS

This pudding looks nicer in individual
servings, so I use 4 small copper pans,
10-12 cm (4-5 inches) in diameter and 5 cm
(2 inches) deep. You could, of course, use
one large pan instead and cut the tatin into
wedges to serve.

225 g (8 oz) butter
225 g (8 oz) caster sugar
6 small pears
225 g (8 oz) ready-made puff pastry

To Serve:
double cream

Spread a quarter of the butter on the
base of each pan and sprinkle with the
sugar. Halve, peel and core the pears
and place three pear halves upside
down in each pan.

Roll out the pastry to a 3 mm (⅛ inch)
thickness and cut out 4 circles, 1 cm
(½ inch) larger than the pan size. Prick
all over with a fork. Place the pastry
circles over the pears and tuck the rim of
the pastry inside each pan.

Place the pans over a low heat to melt
the butter, then increase the heat and
cook until the filling is bubbling and
caramelised to a rich golden brown.
Transfer to a preheated oven at 190°C
(375°F) mark 5 and bake for 20 minutes.
Shake the pans to loosen the filling
before turning out on to individual
plates. Serve with cream.

THE FIRST
SEMI-FINAL
VANESSA BINNS • NICHOLAS HOCKING • NANCY SMITH

WINNER

VANESSA BINNS' MENU

STARTER
*Aubergines layered with Tomato, Feta and Basil, served
with Two Sauces*
"QUITE LIKE A PICASSO PAINTING" LESLIE THOMAS
"DOESN'T PULL ANY PUNCHES" LOYD

MAIN COURSE
*Breast of Guinea Fowl poached in Tea with Morels
Chive and Nutmeg Crêpes filled with Spinach*

DESSERT
Warm Pear Tartlets with Pear Sorbet and Tuiles Butterflies

Aubergines Layered with Tomato, Feta and Basil, and Two Sauces

4 small aubergines
salt and freshly ground black pepper
90 ml (6 tbsp) olive oil
30 g (1 oz) butter
300 g (10 oz) good ripe tomatoes, blanched,
    peeled, seeded and coarsely chopped
pinch of sugar
30 g (1 oz) basil leaves, finely shredded
120 g (4 oz) Greek feta cheese

Tomato Sauce:
15 g (½ oz) butter
200 g (7 oz) can chopped tomatoes
pinch of sugar

Yogurt Sauce:
150 ml (¼ pint) natural yogurt
lemon juice to taste

To Garnish:
few small basil leaves

Cut the aubergines into 1 cm (½ inch) slices. Season with pepper. Heat the olive oil in a frying pan until smoking, then quickly fry the aubergine slices on both sides; drain on kitchen paper.

Melt the butter in a frying pan, add the tomatoes and cook for 1 minute. Add the sugar and basil and season to taste with pepper. Crumble the cheese into the pan and remove from the heat.

Layer the tomato mixture with the aubergine slices in an ovenproof dish and bake in a preheated oven at 200°C (400°F) mark 6 for 7-10 minutes.

Meanwhile, to make the tomato sauce, melt the butter in a pan, add the chopped tomatoes, seasoning and sugar. Cook until reduced by half, then strain through a fine sieve.

For the yogurt sauce, mix the yogurt with a little lemon juice to taste. Serve the terrine with the two sauces.

Breast of Guinea Fowl Poached in Tea with Morels

400 ml (14 fl oz) homemade chicken or
    guinea fowl stock
15 ml (1 tbsp) Earl Grey tea leaves
5 ml (1 tsp) Lapsang Souchong tea leaves
4 guinea fowl breasts, skinned
280 ml (9 fl oz) double cream
20 small morels, fresh or reconstituted dried
    ones
salt and freshly ground black pepper

Bring the stock to the boil in a saucepan. Put the tea leaves into a bowl or jug, add the boiling stock, cover and allow to stand for 10 minutes. Strain into a heavy-based saucepan large enough to hold the guinea fowl breasts.

Bring the stock to a gentle simmer, then add the guinea fowl breasts. Poach gently for about 7 minutes. Remove and wrap loosely in foil; keep warm. Increase the heat and reduce the stock by half. Add the cream and reduce again until the sauce thickens. Add the morels and heat through. Check the seasoning.

Slice the guinea fowl breasts and arrange on warmed serving plates. Coat with the morel sauce. Serve with the spinach-filled crêpes.

CHIVE AND NUTMEG CRÊPES FILLED WITH SPINACH

Crêpes:
56 g (2 oz) plain flour
1 egg
pinch of salt
2.5 ml (½ tsp) freshly grated nutmeg
140 ml (4½ fl oz) milk
30 ml (2 tbsp) snipped chives
14 g (½ oz) melted butter
butter or vegetable oil for frying
beaten egg to seal

Filling:
300 g (10 oz) trimmed spinach leaves
50 g (2 oz) butter
salt and freshly ground black pepper
28 g (1 oz) chopped walnuts (optional)

To make the crêpe batter, in a bowl mix the flour, egg, salt and nutmeg together to a smooth paste. Gradually add the milk until you have a batter the consistency of cream. Allow to stand for 15 minutes. Stir in the chives and melted butter.

Heat a little butter or oil in a crêpe pan, add a little of the batter and tilt the pan to spread evenly and make a 10 cm (4 inch) crêpe. Cook until the underside is golden, then turn and cook the other side. Repeat with the remaining batter to make 8 crêpes, stacking them interleaved with greaseproof paper as they are cooked.

Wash the spinach well. Cook in a covered pan with just the water clinging to the leaves after washing until tender; drain if necessary. Chop the spinach then reheat with a little butter; add seasoning to taste. Add the chopped walnuts if preferred.

Divide the spinach leaves between the crêpes, folding each one over to form a semi-circle. Seal the edges with a little beaten egg. Reheat in a moderate oven at 160°C (325°F) mark 3 for 10 minutes before serving.

WARM PEAR TARTS WITH PEAR SORBET

Pear Sorbet:
3 Anjou Red or William pears
juice of 1 lemon, plus extra for sprinkling
80 g (3 oz) caster sugar
30 ml (2 tbsp) eau-de-vie Poire Williem

Tarts:
350 g (12 oz) puff pastry (preferably made
  with butter)
4 Anjou Red or William pears
lemon juice for sprinkling
110 g (4 oz) unsalted butter
110 g (4 oz) caster sugar

To Finish:
4 tuiles butterflies (see right)

To make the pear sorbet, peel, core and quarter the pears, then coat with lemon juice to prevent discolouration. Place in a saucepan with the sugar. Add sufficient water to half cover and poach gently for 10 minutes.

Remove the pears with a slotted spoon and allow to cool. Reduce the cooking juices until syrupy, then cool. When the pears and syrup are cold, purée them in a food processor or blender, with the juice of 1 lemon and the Poire Williem eau-de-vie.

Transfer the pear purée to an ice-cream maker and freeze. If you do not have an ice cream machine, freeze in a suitable container, beating occasionally to break down the ice crystals.

To make the tarts, roll out the pastry to a rectangle 3 mm (⅛ inch) thick and large enough to cut out 4 circles, 14 cm (5½ inches) in diameter. Cover and place in the freezer for about 10 minutes.

Peel the pears, cut in half and remove the cores. Cut lengthways into 3 mm (⅛ inch) thick slices. Sprinkle all cut surfaces with lemon juice, to prevent discolouration.

Mark a concentric circle 1 cm (½ inch) in from the edge of each pastry round, making sure you only cut halfway through the pastry. Arrange the pear slices, like overlapping petals, within the marked circles. Dot each tart with 15 g (½ oz) of the butter and sprinkle on 15 g (½ oz) of the sugar.

Bake the tarts in a preheated oven at 220°C (425°C) mark 7 for 30 minutes, dotting with the remaining butter and sprinkling with the rest of the sugar halfway through cooking. The pears should be slightly caramelised.

To serve, place a pear tart on each serving plate, position a scoop of sorbet in the middle and top with a tuiles butterfly. Serve immediately.

TUILES BUTTERFLIES

1 egg white
50 g (2 oz) icing sugar
30 g (1¼ oz) butter, softened
40 g (1½ oz) plain flour

Lightly mix the egg white and icing sugar together in a bowl, but do not aerate. Mix in the softened butter and flour to make a smooth firm paste.

Pipe the mixture into butterfly shapes on a baking sheet lined with non-stick baking parchment. Bake in a preheated oven at 160°C (325°F) mark 3 for about 5 minutes until golden brown.

THE FIRST
── SEMI-FINAL ──
VANESSA BINNS • NICHOLAS HOCKING • NANCY SMITH

NICHOLAS HOCKING'S MENU

STARTER
Neufchâtel Cheese with a Caramelised Red Pepper Sauce,
served with a Side Salad and Pumpernickel Bread
"I AM AMAZED THAT SOMETHING AS SWEET AS THIS WORKS AS A STARTER,
BUT IT DOES" DAVID WILSON
"A SURPRISING DISH WHICH KEEPS YOU ON YOUR TOES" LOYD

MAIN COURSE
Grilled Salmon Steaks with a Dill, Cucumber and Green
Peppercorn Sauce, on a bed of Rocket
New Potatoes tossed in Butter and Mint
Broccoli in Sesame Seeds

DESSERT
Ginger Hazelnut Ice Cream served in Brandy Snap Baskets,
with Mango Sauce

NEUFCHÂTEL CHEESE WITH A CARAMELISED RED PEPPER SAUCE

200 g (7 oz) fresh neufchâtel cheese
mixture of salad leaves, eg frisée and lamb's
    lettuce

Dressing:
45 ml (3 tbsp) olive oil
15 ml (1 tbsp) wine vinegar
2.5ml (½ tsp) mustard
salt and freshly ground black pepper
pinch of sugar

Red Pepper Sauce:
125 ml (4 fl oz) dry white wine
125 ml (4 fl oz) vinegar
125 ml (4 fl oz) water
75 g (3 oz) granulated sugar
1 red pepper, cored, seeded and finely
    chopped

To Serve:
pumpernickel bread

Slice the cheese and arrange on individual serving plates with the salad leaves. Combine the ingredients for the dressing in a screw-topped jar and shake vigorously to blend. Spoon a little dressing over the salad leaves.

To make the red pepper sauce, put the wine, vinegar and water in a saucepan. Add the sugar and dissolve over low heat, then increase the heat and reduce by about two thirds until the mixture is forming tiny bubbles; this will take about 10 minutes. Before it begins to caramelise, remove from the heat and add the pepper. Leave for 1 minute, then pour over the cheese.

Let stand for 2 minutes before serving, with pumpernickel bread.

GRILLED SALMON STEAKS WITH A DILL, CUCUMBER AND GREEN PEPPERCORN SAUCE

4 salmon steaks
30 ml (2 tbsp) olive oil
juice of ½ lemon
salt and freshly ground black pepper

Sauce:
10 ml (2 tsp) olive oil
2.5 ml (½ tsp) finely chopped garlic
125 ml (4 fl oz) dry white wine
125 ml (4 fl oz) fish stock
2.5 ml (½ tsp) plain flour
150 ml (5 fl oz) double cream
5 ml (1 tsp) green peppercorns in brine,
    drained
¼ cucumber, peeled, seeded and chopped
75 ml (5 tbsp) chopped dill

To Serve:
rocket leaves

First make the sauce. Heat the oil in a saucepan and lightly fry the chopped garlic, then add the wine and fish stock and reduce by half. Mix the flour with the cream, then add to the sauce and reduce for a further 2 minutes. Add the peppercorns, cucumber, salt, pepper and dill. Set aside.

Brush the salmon steaks liberally with the olive oil and lemon juice. Season with salt and pepper. Grill under a moderately high heat for 8-10 minutes, turning once.

Arrange a bed of rocket leaves on each serving plate. Position a salmon steak on top and pour the sauce over the salmon. Serve with new potatoes tossed in butter and mint, and broccoli flavoured with sesame seeds.

Note: To cook the broccoli steam briefly, then stir-fry in sesame oil over high heat with sesame seeds.

GINGER HAZELNUT ICE CREAM SERVED IN BRANDY SNAP BASKETS WITH MANGO SAUCE

Ice Cream:
50 g (2 oz) shelled hazelnuts
4 pieces preserved stem ginger in syrup
45 ml (3 tbsp) ginger syrup (from the ginger)
175 g (6 oz) caster sugar
125 ml (4 fl oz) water
170 ml (6 fl oz) double cream
125 ml (4 fl oz) single cream
3 egg whites

Mango Sauce:
1 mango
50 g (2 oz) caster sugar
juice of ½ lemon

To Serve:
4 brandy snap baskets (see right)
mint sprigs to decorate

Toast the hazelnuts in a preheated oven at 180°C (350°F) mark 4 for 10 minutes. Allow to cool, then grind in a blender or food processor.

Chop the preserved ginger, then put into a saucepan with the ginger syrup, sugar and water. Place over a low heat until the sugar is dissolved, then cook over a moderate heat for about 10 minutes until reduced by about half. Remove from the heat before the mixture begins to caramelise.

Whip the double and single creams together until they form peaks. In a separate bowl, whisk the egg whites until fairly stiff. Add the nuts and syrup to the whipped cream, then gently fold this mixture into the whisked egg whites.

Transfer to a freezerproof container and freeze for 2-3 hours until semi-frozen. Beat thoroughly to break down the ice crystals, then return to the freezer and freeze until firm.

To make the mango sauce, peel, halve and stone the mango, then purée in a blender or food processor until smooth. Place in a saucepan with the sugar and lemon juice and cook gently for about 5 minutes. Pass through a sieve into a bowl and allow to cool.

To serve, scoop the ice cream into the brandy snap baskets and place on individual plates. Spoon the mango sauce over the ice cream and decorate with mint sprigs to serve.

BRANDY SNAP BASKETS

This quantity is sufficient to make 8 baskets, which should be more than enough to allow for breakages.

75 g (3 oz) unsalted butter
75 g (3 oz) caster sugar
45 ml (3 tbsp) golden syrup
75 g (3 oz) plain flour, sifted

Put the butter, sugar and syrup in a heavy-based saucepan over low heat until dissolved. Remove from the heat and stir in the flour.

Spoon the mixture into 8 large circles on greased baking sheets, spacing well apart. Bake in a preheated oven at 200°C (400°F) mark 6 for 8 minutes or until beginning to brown. Leave for a few moments, then carefully remove with a palette knife and mould each one over an upturned small tumbler. Allow to set, then carefully remove the baskets.

THE FIRST
SEMI-FINAL
Vanessa Binns • Nicholas Hocking • Nancy Smith

NANCY SMITH'S MENU

STARTER
Cream of Chicken and Spinach Soup with Almonds

MAIN COURSE
*Halibut baked in a Mustard and Mushroom Crust with
a Lemon Butter Sauce
Potato Straws
Glazed Baby Carrots*
"IF YOU LIKE FISH AND CHIPS THIS IS A GREAT DISH" LOYD

DESSERT
*Steamed Vanilla and Apricot Puddings, served with
a Fruit Coulis*
"BIG SUCCESS THIS. THE TRAGEDY IS THAT WE ALWAYS HAVE
TO MOVE ALONG" LESLIE THOMAS

CREAM OF CHICKEN AND SPINACH SOUP WITH ALMONDS

100 g (4 oz) butter
2 onions, chopped
450 g (1 lb) fresh spinach, thoroughly
  washed and dried
225 g (8 oz) cooked chicken, chopped
1.5 litres (2½ pints) chicken stock
salt and freshly ground black pepper
15 ml (1 tbsp) lemon juice
2 bay leaves
5 ml (1 tsp) almond essence
25 g (1 oz) flour
60 ml (4 tbsp) double cream

To Garnish:
a little double cream
toasted flaked almonds

Melt half the butter in a large saucepan, add the onions and fry until soft. Add the spinach and sauté for 5 minutes. Add the chicken, stock, salt, pepper, lemon juice, bay leaves and almond essence. Bring to the boil, cover and simmer for 20 minutes. Allow to cool slightly, then purée the soup in a blender or food processor.

Melt the remaining butter in a saucepan, stir in the flour and cook, stirring, for 1 minute. Slowly add the puréed soup and bring to the boil. Simmer gently for 5 minutes. Meanwhile boil the double cream to thin slightly, then stir into the soup.

Divide between warmed soup bowls, swirl in the cream and sprinkle with toasted almonds to serve.

HALIBUT BAKED IN A MUSTARD AND MUSHROOM CRUST WITH LEMON BUTTER SAUCE

50 g (2 oz) fresh breadcrumbs
30 ml (2 tbsp) coarse-grain mustard
100 g (4 oz) mushrooms, finely chopped
15 ml (1 tbsp) chopped parsley
salt and freshly ground white pepper
4 halibut steaks
1 egg, beaten
450 ml (¾ pint) fish stock
75 g (3 oz) butter, cubed
1 glass white wine
1 shallot, chopped
15 ml (1 tbsp) lemon juice

Mix the breadcrumbs with the mustard, mushrooms, parsley, salt and pepper.

Place the fish steaks in a buttered baking tin. Brush the tops with beaten egg, then spread with the mushroom and mustard mixture. Pour in 300 ml (½ pint) of the fish stock and dot with half of the butter. Bake, uncovered, in a preheated oven at 220°C (425°F) mark 7 for 20-30 minutes until the fish is cooked.

Meanwhile, prepare the sauce. Place the wine, shallot and pepper in a small pan and simmer to reduce by about half, then gradually add the remaining 150 ml (¼ pint) fish stock and lemon juice. Bring to the boil, stirring all the time. Simmer for 10 minutes until reduced and thickened, then pass through a sieve. Whisk in the remaining butter, a piece at a time; keep warm.

Transfer the cooked halibut to warmed serving plates and pour the sauce around them. Serve with glazed baby carrots and potato straws.

Note: To make the potato straws, simply deep-fry julienne of potato until crisp and golden.

STEAMED VANILLA AND APRICOT PUDDINGS WITH A FRUIT COULIS

40 g (1½ oz) caster sugar
300 ml (½ pint) water
225 g (8 oz) fresh apricots, stoned and chopped
1 vanilla pod

Sponge mixture:
75 g (3 oz) self-raising flour
5 ml (1 tsp) baking powder
pinch of salt
75 g (3 oz) butter
75 g (3 oz) caster sugar
1 small egg, size 5 or 6
90-120 ml (6-8 tbsp) milk

In a saucepan, dissolve the sugar in the water over low heat. Add the chopped apricots and vanilla pod and poach for 5 minutes; discard the vanilla pod. Remove the apricots with a slotted spoon and set aside. Reduce the liquid to a syrup by fast boiling and reserve.

Put a few pieces of apricot in the base of 4 buttered dariole moulds.

To make the sponge mixture, sift the flour, baking powder and salt together. Cream the butter with the sugar until light and fluffy, then beat in the egg. Fold in half of the chopped apricots. Fold in the flour mixture with enough milk to give a soft dropping consistency.

Spoon into the dariole moulds and cover tightly with foil. Place in a saucepan, containing enough boiling water to come halfway up the sides of the moulds. Steam for 1 hour, topping up with boiling water as necessary.

Purée the remaining fruit in a food processor or blender and mix with the syrup to make the coulis. Turn out the vanilla puddings and serve surrounded by the apricot coulis.

THE SECOND
SEMI-FINAL
LINDA YEWDALL • SARAH GILES • ORLANDO MURRIN

WINNER

LINDA YEWDALL'S MENU

STARTER
Spinach and Anchovy Pâté with Wholemeal Soldiers

MAIN COURSE
Pheasant Pie with Potato Pastry
Creamed Butter Beans
Carrots flavoured with Caraway
Broccoli Purée
"THAT IS WONDERFUL. NOURISHING AND WONDERFUL" SUE LAWLEY

DESSERT
Lemon and Lavender Sorbet
"NICE AND CREAMY ISN'T IT? TICKLES YOUR THROAT. A GOOD
EXPERIENCE" ANTON EDELMANN.

"SCRUMMY" LOYD

SPINACH AND ANCHOVY PÂTÉ WITH WHOLEMEAL SOLDIERS

For this pâté I use 'olde york' ewe's milk cheese, flavoured with garlic and parsley. It has a delicious flavour and a texture like feta. If you cannot obtain it, use cream cheese instead.

350 g (12 oz) spinach leaves
50 g (1¾ oz) anchovies in oil
100 g (4 oz) 'olde york' ewe's milk cheese or cream cheese
squeeze of orange juice
freshly ground black pepper

To Serve:
orange slices and parsley sprigs to garnish
wholemeal toast soldiers

Carefully wash the spinach and remove the tough stalks. Cook in a covered saucepan, with just the water clinging to the leaves after washing, until tender. Finely chop the cooked spinach.

In another saucepan cook the anchovies in their oil for a few minutes, mashing them to a paste. Add the chopped spinach and cook gently until all excess moisture has evaporated. Allow to cool, then mix with the soft cheese, orange juice and pepper to taste. Pot in a ramekin.

Serve garnished with orange slices and parsley, and accompanied by wholemeal toast 'soldiers'.

PHEASANT PIE WITH POTATO PASTRY

This pastry is deliciously short and well worth the effort. You can of course use cold leftover potatoes if you have some.

1 cock pheasant
25 g (1 oz) butter
100 g (4 oz) British smoked bacon rashers, derinded and chopped
1 onion, sliced
1 Bramley apple, peeled, cored and sliced
450 ml (¾ pint) cider
bouquet garni, ie sprig each of marjoram, parsley and thyme
4 cloves
salt and freshly ground black pepper
squeeze of lemon juice

Potato Pastry:
175 g (6 oz) self-raising flour
125 g (4 oz) butter
175 g (6 oz) cold mashed potato
beaten egg for brushing

Carefully remove the breasts and legs from the pheasant. (Use the rest of the meat and carcass to make stock for another dish.) Slice the meat, discarding the bones.

Heat the butter in a heavy-based pan and fry the bacon and onion until golden. Add the pheasant slices together with the apple and fry turning for a few minutes. Add the cider, bouquet garni, cloves, seasoning and lemon juice. Cover and cook for 45 minutes to 1 hour until the pheasant is tender. Discard the bouquet garni.

Meanwhile make the potato pastry. Sift the flour into a bowl, rub in the butter until the mixture resembles breadcrumbs, then add the mashed potato to bind the pastry. Wrap and leave to rest in the refrigerator for about 15 minutes.

Transfer the pheasant mixture to a pie dish. Roll out the pastry on a lightly floured surface to make a pie lid. Moisten the rim of the pie dish and position the pastry over the meat. Decorate the top of the pie with shapes cut from the trimmings. Brush with beaten egg and cook in a preheated oven at 200°C (400°F) mark 6 for 25 minutes. Serve immediately, with the vegetable accompaniments.

Pheasant Stock: Make this from the leftover pheasant carcass and use to cook the butter beans. Put the pheasant carcass in a saucepan or pressure cooker with water to cover and flavouring ingredients - 1 onion, 1 leek, 1 carrot, chopped; 1 clove garlic, crushed; and seasoning. Bring to the boil and cook for 1½ hours, or 30 minutes in a pressure cooker. Strain before using.

CREAMED BUTTER BEANS

I use stock made from the leftover pheasant carcass to cook the butter beans.

225 g (8 oz) butter beans, soaked overnight
900 ml (1½ pints) well-flavoured stock,
*   preferably pheasant*
15 g (½ oz) butter
salt and freshly ground black pepper
snipped chives to garnish

Drain the butter beans and rinse in cold water removing any floating husks; drain. Place in a saucepan with the stock, bring to the boil, lower the heat, cover and cook for about 40 minutes until tender. Strain off the stock and reduce to thicken and concentrate the flavour.

Meanwhile purée the butter beans in a food processor or blender. Return to the cleaned pan and add a little of the concentrated stock with the butter and seasoning. Reheat gently, adding a little more stock if necessary, to obtain the desired consistency.

Sprinkle with snipped chives to serve.

CARROTS WITH CARAWAY

350 g (12 oz) carrots, cut into julienne
*   strips*
2.5 ml (½ tsp) caraway seeds
15 g (½ oz) butter
salt and freshly ground black pepper

Steam the carrots until just tender (or cook in boiling salted water and drain well).

Melt the butter and toss the carrots with the caraway seeds in the melted butter to coat thoroughly. Season with salt and pepper, and serve.

BROCCOLI PURÉE

700 g (1½ lb) broccoli
2 medium potatoes, cut into even-sized
*   pieces*
30 ml (2 tbsp) Greek-style yogurt
tiny knob of butter
squeeze of lime juice
salt and freshly ground black pepper

Divide the broccoli into florets, discarding the stalks. Steam the potatoes and broccoli separately until just tender (or cook in boiling salted water and drain well). Dry the vegetables in a saucepan over gentle heat, then mash until smooth. Add the yogurt, butter, lime juice and salt and pepper to taste. Serve immediately.

Note: Alternatively, you can purée the vegetables in a food processor but take care to avoid overmixing otherwise the texture of the purée will be rather unpleasant.

LEMON AND LAVENDER SORBET

Once it reaches the correct consistency
this sorbet can be left in the freezer until
required, but it is at its best served the day
it is made.

3 lemons
175 g (6 oz) sugar
300 ml (½ pint) water
6 drops of Culpeper's lavender water
1 egg white

To Decorate:
shredded lemon zest
lavender flowers and leaves (optional)

Thinly pare the rinds from two of the
lemons and place in a saucepan with the
sugar and water. Heat gently until the
sugar is dissolved, then simmer for
5 minutes. Remove the lemon rind and
allow to cool.

Squeeze the juice from all 3 lemons
and add to the syrup with the lavender
water. Transfer to a suitable container
and freeze, stirring occasionally. When
the mixture is half-frozen, whisk to
break down the ice crystals. Whisk the
egg white until stiff, then fold into the
half-frozen sorbet. Freeze, stirring
occasionally, until the sorbet resembles
firm snow.

Serve scooped into glass dishes,
decorated with lemon zest, lavender
flowers and leaves if available.

THE SECOND
SEMI-FINAL
LINDA YEWDALL • SARAH GILES • ORLANDO MURRIN

SARAH GILES' MENU

STARTER
Mussels au Gratin
"I THINK I MUST HAVE ANOTHER ONE" ANTON EDELMANN

MAIN COURSE
Roast Duck Breasts in Brandy Sauce with
'Tanfield' Mushrooms
Sautéed Potatoes
Baked Cherry Tomatoes

DESSERT
Rhubarb and Elderflower Syllabub with
Shortbread Hearts

MUSSELS AU GRATIN

Allow 6 mussels per person, but cook a few extra ones to allow for any which do not open up on cooking.

24-30 mussels
1 onion, chopped
few parsley sprigs
1 thyme sprig
50 g (2 oz) butter
5 ml (1 tsp) lemon juice
1 clove garlic, crushed
30 ml (2 tbsp) chopped parsley
25 g (1 oz) white breadcrumbs
25 g (1 oz) freshly grated Parmesan cheese

Scrub the mussels clean under running cold water and discard any with open or cracked shells. Put the onion, parsley and thyme in a saucepan with 300 ml (½ pint) water and bring to the boil. Simmer, covered, for 5 minutes. Add the mussels and cook quickly, shaking the pan constantly until the shells open. Remove from the heat and discard any mussels which have not opened. Leave to cool slightly.

Discard the empty half shells and arrange the mussels in individual gratin dishes. Melt the butter and stir in the lemon juice and garlic. Spoon the flavoured butter over the mussels and scatter over the parsley. Mix the breadcrumbs and Parmesan together and sprinkle over the top. Cook under a preheated grill for about 3 minutes until golden. Serve immediately.

ROAST DUCK BREASTS IN BRANDY SAUCE

3 Lincolnshire duckling breasts
45 ml (3 tbsp) clear honey
300 ml (½ pint) chicken stock
45 ml (3 tbsp) brandy
5 ml (1 tsp) redcurrant jelly
salt and freshly ground black pepper

Spread the honey over the duckling skins and place in a roasting tin, skin side up. Leave for about 30 minutes, then roast in a preheated oven at 210°C (410°F) mark 6½ for about 25 minutes.

Meanwhile heat the stock in a saucepan and reduce by half, then add the brandy and redcurrant jelly and stir over a low heat until dissolved. Season with salt and pepper to taste.

Carve the duckling breasts and arrange in a fan on each plate. Pour a little sauce over them and serve with 'Tanfield' mushrooms, sautéed potatoes and baked cherry tomatoes.

Note: To bake cherry tomatoes, pierce the skins to prevent them bursting and cook in a preheated oven at 190°C (375°F) mark 5 for about 20 minutes.

'TANFIELD' MUSHROOMS

4 chestnut mushrooms
½ small chicken breast fillet
25 ml (1 fl oz) double cream
1 egg white
½ clove garlic, crushed
sprinkling of dried mixed herbs
salt and freshly ground black pepper

Peel the mushrooms, then remove and chop the stalks. Roughly chop the chicken and mix with the mushroom stalks, cream, egg white, garlic, herbs and seasoning. Purée in a blender or food processor until smooth, then use to stuff the mushroom caps.

Bake in the roasting tin (with the duckling breasts) at 210°C (410°F) mark 6½ for 25 minutes.

Rhubarb and Elderflower Syllabub with Shortbread Hearts

6 stalks rhubarb
60 ml (2 fl oz) elderflower wine
50 g (2 oz) caster sugar
5 ml (1 tsp) ground ginger
10 ml (2 tsp) arrowroot

Syllabub:
300 ml (½ pint) double cream
90 ml (6 tbsp) elderflower wine
squeeze of lemon juice
50 g (2 oz) caster sugar
5 ml (1 tsp) brandy

Shortbread:
50 g (2 oz) butter
50 g (2 oz) caster sugar
few drops of vanilla essence
50 g (2 oz) plain flour
25 g (1 oz) self-raising flour
icing sugar for dusting

Cut the rhubarb into 2.5 cm (1 inch) pieces and place in a heavy-based saucepan with the wine, sugar and ginger. Bring to the boil, lower the heat and simmer until tender. Mix the arrowroot with a little cold water until smooth, then stir into the rhubarb mixture. Heat, stirring, until slightly thickened. Allow to cool.

Spoon the rhubarb into the base of 4 tall glasses, reserving 45 ml (3 tbsp) of the mixture for the syllabub.

To make the syllabub, whip the cream until thick, then whisk in the wine, lemon juice, sugar and brandy. Stir in the reserved rhubarb mixture and spoon in to the glasses. Chill until required.

To make the shortbread, cream the butter with the sugar and vanilla essence. Stir in the plain and self-raising flours. Shape into a ball and leave to rest for 30 minutes. Roll out thinly and cut out heart shapes, using a suitable cutter. Bake in a preheated oven at 180°C (350°F) mark 4 for 10 minutes until pale golden. Immediately transfer to a wire rack and dust with icing sugar. Allow to cool.

Serve the syllabub dessert with the shortbread hearts.

THE SECOND
SEMI-FINAL
LINDA YEWDALL • SARAH GILES • ORLANDO MURRIN

ORLANDO MURRIN'S MENU

STARTER
Warm Salad of Fragrant Mussels

MAIN COURSE
Salt-roast Duck with Caramel Sauce
French Potato Cake
Creamed Spinach and Sorrel
"THAT IS CLEVER, LOVELY COMBINATION" SUE LAWLEY
"VERY WELL JUGGLED" LOYD

DESSERT
Iced Ginger Bombes with Vanilla Stars
"VERY GOOD BALANCE. ABSOLUTELY WONDERFUL" SUE LAWLEY

WARM SALAD OF FRAGRANT MUSSELS

A simple, pretty and stylish starter with a
captivating texture.

1-1.4 kg (2-3 lb) mussels
2 shallots, chopped
125 ml (4 fl oz) white wine
freshly ground pepper
lemon juice to taste
2 carrots, cut into matchsticks

Sauce:
pinch of saffron
pinch of curry powder (your own blend, or
    bought)
90 ml (3 fl oz) double cream
40 g (1½ oz) butter, in pieces

To Finish:
1 small curly endive
45 ml (3 tbsp) finely snipped chives
pinch of garam masala (your own blend, or
    bought)

Scrub the mussels thoroughly under
running cold water and remove their
beards. Put the mussels on a rack in a
large roasting tin. Sprinkle with the
shallots and white wine and cover
tightly with foil. Bake in a preheated
oven at 240°C (475°F) mark 9 for 8-10
minutes, depending on size, until they
open.

Meanwhile, blanch the carrots in
boiling water for 30 seconds. Drain,
rinse in cold water and drain.

Remove the mussels from their shells,
catching the juices in the roasting tin
and discarding any that have not
opened. Put the mussels in a bowl,
sprinkle with pepper and a little lemon
juice and keep warm.

To make the sauce, carefully strain the
mussel cooking liquid through a very
fine sieve or a couple of thicknesses of
muslin into a pan. Add the saffron and
curry powder and reduce by half; strain
again. Mix in the cream and simmer
until the sauce is thick enough to just
coat the back of a spoon. Swirl in the
butter to thicken.

Roll up the curly endive and cut into
fine strips. Add to the sauce with the
mussels, carrots, and most of the chives.
Check the seasoning and add lemon
juice if wished. Keep warm but do not
boil. Arrange decoratively on warmed
plates, finishing with a few chives and a
dusting of garam masala.

Maryland Crab Cakes with Tartare Sauce and Salad
MARTHA SPENCER'S STARTER (SEMI-FINAL)

Southdown Lamb Fillet with Garlic Sauce and accompaniments
VANESSA BINNS' MAIN COURSE (FINAL)

SALT-ROAST DUCK WITH CARAMEL SAUCE

This is a remarkable and totally reliable way of cooking duck to perfection. The salt draws out all the fat from the meat, and the flavour is magical – not at all salty. The glistening caramel sauce is richly flavoured – not at all of vinegar – and quite unlike any other! Buy a whole duck and use the rest of the carcass to make the stock for the sauce.

2 duck breasts, with skin
freshly ground black pepper
1.4 kg (3 lb) coarse sea salt
6 egg whites
freshly ground pepper

Caramel Sauce:
45 ml (3 tbsp) sugar
250 ml (8 fl oz) red wine vinegar
300 ml (½ pint) strong duck stock
150 ml (¼ pint) double cream

Score shallow crosses in the skin of the duck breasts with a sharp knife. Heat a heavy-based frying pan and brown the duck breasts, one at a time, skin side down, for 3 minutes, then remove. Sprinkle the duck breasts with pepper and reform into their original shape by tying at each end with string.

Mix the sea salt with the egg whites and put a thin layer in the base of two 1 kg (2 lb) loaf tins. Put a duck breast in each tin and cover completely with more salt. Roast immediately in a preheated oven at 230°C (450°F) mark 8 for 17 minutes. Remove and let stand for 10 minutes.

Meanwhile, make the caramel sauce. In a deep saucepan, dissolve the sugar in the vinegar over low heat, then increase the heat and cook to a caramel, about 10 minutes. Mix in the stock and bring to the boil. Add the cream, but do not stir! Boil vigorously for 5-8 minutes, or until the sauce is boiling with small bubbles; the stronger your stock, the quicker this will happen. Stir gently and remove from the heat. Season with a little pepper. Keep warm over a saucepan of hot water.

Break open the salt crust and take out the duck breasts. Wipe off the salt with paper towels, remove the duck skin, then thinly slice the duck breasts and serve with pepper.

Note: The duck breasts release a large amount of fat when they are browned. You can use this duck fat for the French potato cake if you like.

FRENCH POTATO CAKE

A sensational way to bring out the succulent aromatic pleasure of potatoes.

30 ml (2 tbsp) butter or duck fat
600 g (1¼ lb) potatoes, peeled and thinly
  sliced
2.5 ml (½ tsp) salt
freshly ground pepper
15 g (½ oz) butter, plus extra for greasing
2 garlic cloves, finely chopped
30 ml (2 tbsp) finely chopped parsley

Heat the fat in a heavy-based frying pan and fry the potatoes, partially covered, until lightly browned, about 25 minutes. Season with salt and pepper.

Pack the potatoes into a buttered shallow tart tin or individual flan tins, pressing down firmly. Bake in a preheated oven at 200°C (400°F) mark 6 for about 20 minutes, or until brown and slightly puffy.

Drizzle butter around the edge of the tin, loosen the potato cake and turn out. Cut into wedges and sprinkle with the garlic and parsley to serve.

CREAMED SPINACH AND SORREL

If you can't get hold of this quantity of sorrel, simply make up the difference with spinach.

450 g (1 lb) spinach
100 g (4 oz) sorrel
25 g (1 oz) butter
2.5 ml (½ tsp) salt
1.25 ml (¼ tsp) freshly ground pepper
5 ml (1 tsp) cream

Wash the spinach and remove the tough stalks. Cook the spinach in a large covered pan with just the water clinging to the leaves after washing until tender. Whizz in a food processor or blender until smooth.

Meanwhile, wash the sorrel, discard the stems and cut into fine strips. Melt the butter in a pan, add the sorrel and seasoning and cook for about 5 minutes until all moisture has evaporated. Add the puréed spinach and cream and heat through.

ICED GINGER BOMBES

These are very pretty frozen in individual bombe moulds but, if you don't have any, use a shallow cake tin instead. To save time, you could use ready-made meringues – very lightly toasted. You will need 65 g (2½ oz).

2 egg whites
100 g (4 oz) caster sugar

To Assemble:
250 ml (8 fl oz) double cream
grated rind of 1 lemon
30 ml (2 tbsp) kirsch
15 ml (1 tbsp) caster sugar
45 ml (3 tbsp) marinated ginger and
*   crystallised fruits (see note)*

To Serve:
few preserved stem ginger slices
kirsch for sprinkling

To make the meringues, whisk the egg whites until stiff, then gradually whisk in half of the sugar a spoonful at a time. Fold in the rest of the sugar, using a metal spoon, to yield a firm, glossy meringue. Spoon into small mounds on a baking sheet lined with non-stick baking parchment. Bake in a preheated oven at 95°C (200°F) barely mark ¼ for 2 hours. Transfer to a wire rack to cool.

Line 4 individual bombe moulds with cling film. Break up the meringues roughly. Whisk the cream until fairly stiff, then fold in the meringues together with the remaining ingredients. Divide between the moulds; freeze until firm.

Turn the iced bombes out on to plates and top with a little ginger and kirsch.

Note: I keep a jar of sliced preserved stem ginger, crystallised pineapple and sultanas macerating in brandy in my refrigerator. Chopped up, they add a luxurious touch to desserts.

VANILLA STARS

These melt in the mouth, but also under the rolling pin, so handle the dough very carefully! You may find it easier to roll it between sheets of lightly floured non-stick baking parchment.

100 g (4 oz) unsalted butter, chilled
50 g (2 oz) icing sugar
75 g (3 oz) plain flour
25 g (1 oz) cornflour
pinch of baking powder
pinch of salt
1 moist vanilla pod, seeds and pulp extracted

Cream the butter with the icing sugar in a food processor. Sift the dry ingredients together and add to the creamed mixture with the vanilla pulp and seeds. Work briefly, until the dough begins to hold together. Chill in the refrigerator for about 30 minutes.

Carefully roll out the dough to 5 mm (¼ inch) thickness. Cut out stars, using a suitable cutter, prick with a fork and place on a baking sheet. Bake in a preheated oven at 180°C (350°F) mark 4 for 15-20 minutes until pale golden brown. Cool on a wire rack. Serve with the iced ginger bombes.

Note: This quantity makes about 15 vanilla stars.

THE THIRD

SEMI-FINAL

MARTHA SPENCER • GREGORY LEWIS • TIM SOUSTER

WINNER

MARTHA SPENCER'S MENU

STARTER

Maryland Crabcakes with Tartare Sauce, served with a Green Salad

"CERTAINLY AS GOOD AS ANY CRABCAKE I HAVE EATEN" LOYD

MAIN COURSE

Grilled Breast of Duck in Red Wine Sauce, served with Potato and Wild Mushroom Cakes

Seasonal Vegetables

"IF YOU GOT THAT IN A RESTAURANT YOU WOULD FEEL YOU HAD DONE WELL" ANDREW NEIL

DESSERT

Lemon Sponge Custard with Raspberry Coulis

"SIMILAR TO A VERY RICH LEMON CURD" LOYD

MARYLAND CRABCAKES WITH TARTARE SAUCE

Crab Cakes:
1 large egg
22 ml (1½ tbsp) double cream
7.5 ml (1½ tsp) Dijon mustard
2.5 ml (½ tsp) Worcestershire sauce
5 ml (1 tsp) Old Bay seasoning
pinch of cayenne pepper
freshly ground pepper
22 ml (1½ tbsp) minced spring onions
15 ml (1 tbsp) minced fresh parsley
60 ml (4 tbsp) mayonnaise
450 g (1 lb) crabmeat
22 ml (1½ tbsp) ground almonds
50 g (2 oz) fine breadcrumbs
225 g (8 oz) clarified butter

Tartare Sauce:
15 ml (1 tbsp) Champagne vinegar
7.5 ml (1½ tsp) Dijon mustard
pinch of salt
freshly ground pepper
Tabasco sauce to taste
125 ml (4 fl oz) mayonnaise
½ medium onion, finely chopped
30 ml (2 tbsp) finely chopped dill pickles
30 ml (2 tbsp) finely chopped parsley
7.5 ml (1½ tsp) finely chopped chives
15 ml (1 tbsp) chopped capers

To Garnish:
60 ml (4 tbsp) finely chopped parsley

To make the crab cakes, lightly whisk the egg in a large mixing bowl, then add the cream, mustard, Worcestershire sauce, Old Bay seasoning, cayenne and pepper to taste, and continue whisking until well blended. Add the spring onions, minced parsley and mayonnaise and mix until all of the ingredients are well blended. Gently fold in the crabmeat and ground almonds, taking care to break up the crabmeat as little as possible.

Using the hands, form the mixture into 4 equal-sized cakes and coat each cake lightly with breadcrumbs. Place the crab cakes on a baking sheet, cover and chill for 1 hour.

Meanwhile, make the tartare sauce. Put the vinegar, mustard, salt, pepper and Tabasco in a bowl and whisk until well blended. Add the mayonnaise, onion, pickles, parsley, chives and capers, and beat thoroughly until all of the ingredients are well blended. Cover and chill until required.

Heat the clarified butter in a large, heavy-based frying pan over a moderate heat. Add the crabcakes and sauté for 3-4 minutes on each side until golden brown. Drain on absorbent kitchen paper and keep warm. Sprinkle each cake with chopped parsley and serve accompanied by the tartare sauce and a green salad.

GRILLED BREAST OF DUCK IN RED WINE SAUCE

4 duck breasts, each about 175 g (6 oz), boned (carcasses reserved)
15 ml (1 tbsp) each finely chopped basil, rosemary, sage and thyme

Sauce:
15 ml (1 tbsp) butter
15 ml (1 tbsp) oil
150 ml (¼ pint) red wine
2 shallots, chopped
15 ml (1 tbsp) tomato purée
30 ml (2 tbsp) brandy
600 ml (1 pint) rich brown poultry stock
beurre manié, ie 15 ml (1 tbsp) butter blended with 15 ml (1 tbsp) flour

To prepare the sauce, chop the duck carcasses into small pieces. Heat the butter and oil in a large pan and add the duck bones. Cook, turning occasionally, until browned. Remove the excess fat from the pan, then deglaze with the red wine, stirring to scrape up the sediment.

Add the chopped shallots, tomato purée and brandy, then flambé. When the flames subside, add the brown poultry stock. Boil to reduce by half. Strain through a sieve lined with a double thickness of muslin, correct the seasoning and return to the cleaned pan. Thicken the sauce with beurre manié, adding it a little at a time, until the sauce reaches a coating consistency. Set aside.

To prepare the duck breasts, remove the tendon from each one. Press the chopped herbs on to the breasts and cook under a preheated grill for about 4 minutes each side until browned on the outside, but still rare in the middle. Leave to rest for 5-10 minutes before carving.

Pour a pool of sauce on to each warmed plate and arrange the duck on top. Serve with the potato and mushroom cakes, and seasonal vegetables.

POTATO AND WILD MUSHROOM CAKES

250 g (9 oz) potatoes, peeled
7 g (¼ oz) dried mushrooms
450 g (1 lb) cultivated mushrooms
30 ml (2 tbsp) butter
30 ml (2 tbsp) oil
185 ml (6 fl oz) double cream
1 clove garlic, chopped
salt and freshly ground black pepper
butter for greasing

Cut the potatoes into 3 mm (⅛ inch) slices and immerse in a bowl of cold water. Soak the dried mushrooms in sufficient hot water to cover for 20 minutes. Drain, reserving the soaking liquid. Cut the cultivated mushrooms into 3 mm (⅛ inch) slices.

Heat the butter and oil in a pan and sauté the cultivated mushrooms to soften. Add the soaked mushrooms and sauté for 1 minute, then add the cream and garlic and reduce again. Season with salt and pepper to taste.

Drain the potatoes and dry well. Melt a knob of butter in the base of each of 4 ramekins. Arrange half of the potatoes in the ramekins in overlapping spirals. Cover with a layer of mushrooms, then top with the remaining potatoes. Dot with butter and bake in a preheated oven at 200°C (400°F) mark 6 for 25-30 minutes. Unmould to serve.

LEMON SPONGE CUSTARD WITH RASPBERRY COULIS

Lemon Sponge:
175 g (6 oz) sugar
20 g (¾ oz) butter
10 ml (2 tsp) finely grated lemon rind
3 eggs, separated
45 ml (3 tbsp) plain flour
60 ml (4 tbsp) lemon juice
125 ml (4 fl oz) milk

Raspberry Coulis:
450 g (1 lb) raspberries
50 g (2 oz) icing sugar

In a bowl, cream the sugar with the butter and lemon rind, then beat in the egg yolks. Fold in the flour, alternately with the lemon juice and milk.

Whisk the egg whites until stiff, but not dry, then fold into the lemon sponge mixture. Divide equally between 4 buttered custard cups and set them on a rack in a roasting tin containing 2.5 cm (1 inch) depth of hot water. Bake in a preheated oven at 180°C (350°F) mark 4 for about 45 minutes.

Meanwhile prepare the coulis. Purée the raspberries in a blender or food processor with the icing sugar, then pass through a sieve to remove the pips.

Unmould the sponge custards and serve with the raspberry coulis.

The Third

Semi-Final

Martha Spencer • Gregory Lewis • Tim Souster

Gregory Lewis' Menu

Starter

Tartare of Haddock with Avocado and Cucumber
"Good, clean, must have another spoonful." Alastair Little

Main Course

Medallions of Beef in a Madeira and Red Wine Sauce, with a Mushroom and Shallot Garnish
Gâteau of Vegetables

Dessert

Honey Wafers with Mascarpone Amaretto Cream and Berries

TARTARE OF HADDOCK WITH AVOCADO AND CUCUMBER

To prepare this starter you will need
4 stainless steel ring moulds or a 5 cm
(2 inch) pastry cutter.

Mayonnaise:
1 egg yolk, size 5
2.5 ml (½ tsp) Dijon mustard
25 ml (5 tsp) groundnut oil
2.5 ml (½ tsp) horseradish sauce (optional)
salt and freshly ground black pepper
dash of lemon juice

Cucumber Garnish:
½ cucumber

Tartare:
80 g (3 oz) cucumber
50 g (2 oz) potato, peeled
125 g (4 oz) lightly smoked haddock
   (undyed)
1 small shallot, finely diced
20 g (¾ oz) red pepper, skinned, seeded and
   diced
20 g (¾ oz) yellow pepper, skinned, seeded
   and diced
5 ml (1 tsp) chopped parsley
2.5 ml (½ tsp) chopped chives

To Garnish:
40 ml (8 tsp) fromage frais or soured cream
a little grated fresh horseradish
2 tomatoes, peeled, seeded and diced
5 ml (1 tsp) champagne vinegar
20 ml (4 tsp) groundnut oil
1 avocado

To make the mayonnaise, mix the egg yolk and mustard together in a bowl. Whisk continuously while adding the oil gradually in a steady stream. Add the horseradish sauce if using. Season with salt and pepper. Add a little lemon juice.

For the cucumber garnish, peel the cucumber, cut in half lengthwise, remove the seeds and slice very thinly. Sprinkle with salt and set aside for 30 minutes.

For the tartare, peel the cucumber, halve lengthwise and remove the seeds. Cut into 3 mm (⅛ inch) dice. Sprinkle with salt and leave for 5 min-utes, then rinse thoroughly and drain on absorbent kitchen paper. Cut the potato into 3 mm (⅛ inch) dice. Boil in salted water for 2-3 minutes until just cooked. Drain, refresh in cold water and drain on kitchen paper. Skin the haddock, then cut into 3 mm (⅛ inch) dice. Mix all the ingredients for the tartare in a bowl. Bind the mixture with 15 ml (1 tbsp) mayonnaise. Taste and adjust seasoning.

To serve, place a metal ring in the centre of each serving plate. Fill with the tartare mixture, pressing down well and leaving a slight hollow in the centre. Remove the metal rings. Spread the fromage frais on top and add a little grated horseradish and chopped tomato.

Combine the champagne vinegar and oil in a screw-topped jar and shake well to combine. Peel, stone and slice the avocado and carefully toss in the vinaigrette, then arrange around the tartare. Rinse the cucumber garnish thoroughly, then drain well and toss in the vinaigrette. Arrange around the avocado slices. Serve immediately.

Note: To skin peppers, grill turning frequently until the skins are blistered. Leave until cool enough to handle, then peel away the skins.

MEDALLIONS OF BEEF IN A MADEIRA AND RED WINE SAUCE, WITH A MUSHROOM AND SHALLOT GARNISH

4 fillet steaks, each about 175 g (6 oz)
5 ml (1 tsp) unsalted butter
5 ml (1 tsp) sunflower oil
salt and freshly ground black pepper

Sauce:
8 shallots, finely chopped
1 thyme sprig
1 bay leaf
50 ml (3½ tbsp) Madeira
50 ml (3½ tbsp) red wine vinegar
400 ml (14 fl oz) full-bodied red wine
300 ml (½ pint) veal stock
100 ml (3½ fl oz) chicken stock
5 g (¼ oz) cold unsalted butter, diced

Shallot Garnish:
32 shallots (or 16 shallots and 16 baby
  onions), topped and tailed
30 g (1 oz) unsalted butter
1 thyme sprig
½ bay leaf
rock salt for baking
pinch of caster sugar

Mushroom Garnish:
50 g (2 oz) unsalted butter
10 ml (2 tsp) finely chopped shallot
225 g (8 oz) assorted mushrooms, cleaned
  and dried
2 tomatoes, peeled, seeded and diced
15 ml (1 tbsp) chopped chives

First make the sauce. Combine all the ingredients in a bowl, except the stock and butter. Add salt and pepper. Leave to infuse for several hours, or preferably overnight if time. Transfer to a saucepan, bring to the boil and reduce by two thirds. Add the stock and reduce by half. Remove the herbs. Add the butter and stir well until combined. Adjust the seasoning if necessary.

To prepare the shallot garnish, put 16 shallots in a foil parcel with 15 g (½ oz) butter, the thyme, bay leaf and a pinch of salt. Place on a bed of rock salt on a baking sheet and bake in a preheated oven at 220°C (425°F) mark 7 for 20-30 minutes until soft and shiny.

Peel the remaining 16 shallots or onions, melt the remaining 15 g (½ oz) butter in a sauté pan, then add the peeled shallots, sugar, salt and pepper. Cook until lightly browned, then cover with buttered greaseproof paper and cook in the oven for 20 minutes, stirring occasionally, until golden brown.

To prepare the mushroom garnish, melt half of the butter in a pan and sweat the shallot until soft but not coloured. Add the mushrooms and cook for 1 minute. If they release a lot of moisture drain in a colander, then return to the pan. Add the remaining butter and cook for a further 1 minute. Just before serving, add the chopped tomatoes and chives.

To cook the steaks, heat the butter and oil in a frying pan and sear the steaks over high heat for 2 minutes on each side, then cook for a further few seconds on each side. Season with salt and pepper. Place in the preheated oven for approximately 6 minutes, for medium rare steaks.

To serve, reheat the sauce. Slice each steak into 4 to 6 slices, depending on size. Arrange on warmed serving plates around the gâteau of vegetables. Add the mushroom and shallot garnishes and pour the sauce around to serve.

GÂTEAU OF VEGETABLES

These individual gâteaux are cooked in loose-based moulds to allow any excess water to drain away. Alternatively you can use rings and seal the bases with pierced foil.

2 carrots, peeled and cut into pieces
salt and freshly ground black pepper
2.5 ml (½ tsp) sugar
25 g (1 oz) unsalted butter, plus a knob
200 g (7 oz) spinach, thoroughly washed and
    drained
1 clove garlic, crushed
20 ml (4 tsp) olive oil
2 tomatoes, peeled, seeded and chopped
2 courgettes, thinly sliced
1 large parsnip, peeled and sliced
2 basil leaves, shredded

Cook the carrots in a little salted water, with the sugar added, until tender. Drain and chop finely or purée in a food processor with a knob of butter.

Melt 15 g (½ oz) butter in a pan. Remove any coarse stalks from the spinach, then add to the pan with the garlic. Cook over a fairly high heat for a few minutes until the spinach is tender and excess moisture has evaporated. Drain on absorbent kitchen paper.

Heat half the olive oil in a pan, add the tomatoes and cook for a few minutes until soft. Fry the courgettes in the remaining olive oil for about 2 minutes until softened.

Parboil the parsnips in salted water for 2-3 minutes. Drain and refresh in cold water. Dry on absorbent kitchen paper, then grate. Mix with the remaining 15 g (½ oz) butter and cook gently until lightly coloured.

Line 4 loose-based 10 cm (4 inch) moulds with foil and pierce the foil in several places. Adjust the seasoning of the vegetables to taste.

To assemble each gâteau, spoon a portion of spinach into the base of each mould and press down well. Add a layer of carrot and press down. Place the courgette slices around the edge, slightly overlapping them to form a well. Add the chopped basil to the tomato and spoon into the well. Fill the moulds to the top with parsnip, pressing down well. Reheat the gâteaux in a steamer, then turn out before serving.

Note: The gâteaux can be reheated in the microwave, but the foil must be removed first.

Honey Wafers with Mascarpone Amaretto Cream and Berries

This quantity is sufficient to make 12 honey wafers. Shape them on 2 baking sheets and bake one sheet at a time.

Honey Wafers:
30 ml (2 tbsp) unsalted butter, softened
40 g (1½ oz) icing sugar, sifted
30 ml (2 tbsp) clear honey
40 g (1½ oz) plain flour, sifted
2.5 ml (½ tsp) ground cinnamon
1 egg white (approximately)

Cream:
150 ml (¼ pint) whipping cream
100 g (4 oz) mascarpone cheese
15 ml (1 tbsp) Amaretto di Saronno liqueur
10 ml (2 tsp) caster sugar

To Assemble:
225 g (8 oz) raspberries, small strawberries or blueberries
icing sugar for dusting

To make the honey wafers, in a bowl cream the butter with the icing sugar, then beat in the honey. Stir in the flour and cinnamon, with enough egg white to give a smooth batter consistency; it must not be too thin.

Spread a teaspoonful of batter into a 7.5 cm (3 inch) round on a baking sheet lined with non-stick baking parchment. Repeat to make 6 wafers, leaving at least a 4 cm (½ inch) space between them. Bake in a preheated oven at 220°C (425°F) mark 7 for about 3 minutes until golden brown. Cool slightly before transferring to a wire rack to cool completely. Repeat to make another 6 wafers.

For the cream, whisk the cream with the mascarpone and liqueur until firm.
To assemble, place one honey wafer on each serving plate. Spread with a layer of cream, then cover with fruit. Add another wafer, spread with more cream and fruit. Top with the final wafer and dust with icing sugar. Decorate the plate with berries to serve.

THE THIRD
SEMI-FINAL
MARTHA SPENCER • GREGORY LEWIS • TIM SOUSTER

TIM SOUSTER'S MENU

STARTER
'Bacon and Eggs'
Rolls of Prosciutto and Westphalian Ham with Scrambled Egg
on Garlic Croûtes
"I LIKE THAT, THAT IS A GOOD BREAKFAST" ALISTAIR LITTLE

MAIN COURSE
'Fish and Chips and Mushy Peas'
Monkfish Tails 'en papillote' with Vinegar and Caper Sauce
Celeriac Chips
Green Pea and Chick Pea Mould

DESSERT
'Strawberry Cream Tea'
Earl Grey Ice Cream on a Strawberry Coulis with
Madeleine Cake

'BACON AND EGGS'

4 slices, cut from a fat baguette, each 4 cm
    (1½ inches) thick
65 g (2½ oz) butter, softened
1 clove garlic, crushed
5 ml (1 tsp) sesame seeds
4 slices prosciutto
4 slices Westphalian ham
4 eggs, lightly beaten
30 ml (2 tbsp) double cream
salt and freshly ground black pepper
25 g (1 oz) Parmesan cheese, freshly grated

Chinese Marmalade Sauce:
15 ml (1 tbsp) orange marmalade
15 ml (1 tbsp) grapefruit marmalade
2.5 ml (½ tsp) finely chopped fresh root
    ginger
10 ml (2 tbsp) Chinese rice wine vinegar

First combine the ingredients for the Chinese marmalade sauce in a small bowl; leave to stand.

Hollow out the baguette slices to form a cavity in each one. Mix 50 g (2 oz) butter with the garlic. Spread the baguette slices with the garlic butter. Toast the sesame seeds on a baking sheet in a preheated oven at 170°C (325°F) mark 3 for 15 minutes. Bake the baguette slices in the oven at 200°C (400°F) mark 6 for 10 minutes or until golden.

Place the croûtes on individual serving plates, with the prosciutto and Westphalian ham slices alongside. Lightly scramble the eggs with the cream, remaining butter and seasoning for about 2 minutes. Spoon the scrambled eggs on to the croûtes and garnish with freshly grated Parmesan and sesame seeds. Serve immediately, with the Chinese marmalade sauce.

'FISH AND CHIPS AND MUSHY PEAS'

Mushy Peas:
100 g (4 oz) chick peas, soaked overnight
100 g (4 oz) peas
1 mint sprig
2 egg yolks
cayenne pepper
freshly grated nutmeg

Papillotes:
4 monkfish tails, on the bone
30 ml (2 tbsp) Chinese rice wine vinegar
60 ml (4 tbsp) double cream
20 capers
salt and freshly ground black pepper

Chips:
1 head celeriac
oil for deep-frying

To Garnish
mint sprigs

Drain the chick peas and place in a saucepan. Add water to cover and simmer for about 1 hour until tender; drain. Cook the peas in boiling water for 2 minutes, then drain. Briefly whizz the chick peas and green peas in a food processor or blender with the mint, egg yolks, cayenne pepper and nutmeg to taste until evenly mixed. Divide the mixture between 4 dariole moulds, cover with foil and steam for about 20 minutes.

To make the papillotes, you will need 4 large squares of foil. Place a portion of fish on each square and sprinkle with the vinegar, cream, capers, salt and pepper. Fold the foil to enclose the fish and form parcels. Bake in a preheated oven at 180°C (350°F) mark 4 for 15 minutes.

Meanwhile, cut the celeriac into small, thin chips. Heat the oil in a deep-fat fryer to 170°C (330°F) and deep-fry the celeriac chips for 5 minutes. Remove and allow to drain for 5 minutes, then deep-fry at 190°C (375°F) for 2 minutes to crisp and brown. Drain on absorbent kitchen paper.

To serve, unwrap the papillotes. Place the fish on warmed plates and garnish with dill. Unmould the 'mushy peas' on to the plates and garnish with mint. Serve with the celeriac chips.

STRAWBERRY CREAM TEA

Sorbet:
15 ml (3 tsp) Earl Grey tea leaves
1 large mint sprig
200 g (7 oz) granulated sugar
450 ml (¾ pint) water
juice of 1 lemon

Coulis:
225 g (8 oz) strawberries
45 ml (3 tbsp) strawberry jam
juice of 1 lemon
125 ml (4 fl oz) double cream

To Decorate:
mint leaves or strawberry slices

Put the tea leaves and mint in a bowl. Put the sugar and water in a saucepan over a low heat until dissolved, then bring to the boil and allow to bubble for 1 minute. Remove from the heat and add the lemon juice. Pour the syrup over the tea mixture, cover and leave to infuse for 3 minutes. Strain into a jug, allow to cool, then chill. Transfer to an ice-cream maker and churn for 20 minutes, then freeze in a suitable container. Alternatively if you do not have an ice cream maker, whisk occasionally during freezing to improve the texture.

To make the coulis, purée the strawberries in a blender or food processor. Add the jam and blend for a few seconds only; otherwise the mixture will become frothy. Stir in the lemon juice. Pass the coulis through a fine chinois (sieve). Spread a pool of coulis on each serving plate and chill thoroughly.

Lightly whip the cream so that it will pour slowly. Pour a circle of cream on to each portion of coulis and feather with a chopstick to decorate. Place two scoops of sorbet in the centre of each plate. Decorate with mint leaves or strawberry slices and serve with the madeleines.

MADELEINES

This quantity makes 12 madeleines.

50 g (2 oz) plain flour
2.5 ml (½ tsp) baking powder
2 eggs
65 g (2½ oz) caster sugar
5 ml (1 tsp) orange flower water
50 g (2 oz) butter, melted

Sift the flour and baking powder together into a bowl. In another bowl, whisk the eggs, then whisk in the sugar until light and creamy. Gradually fold in the flour, a third at a time, adding the orange flower water and melted butter with the final third. Cover and chill for 30 minutes.

Butter and flour a madeleine tin and two-thirds fill each mould with the mixture. Bake in a preheated oven at 230°C (450°F) mark 8 for 5 minutes, then lower the temperature to 200°C (400°F) mark 6 and bake for a further 5 minutes. Transfer to a wire rack to cool.

THE
FINAL

VANESSA BINNS • MARTHA SPENCER • LINDA YEWDALL

——— WINNER ———

VANESSA BINNS' FINAL MENU

STARTER

Smoked Fish Terrine with Buttermere Eel and Two Sauces

"AS GOOD A FISH TERRINE AS I HAVE HAD IN A LONG TIME" LOYD

MAIN COURSE

Southdown Lamb Fillet with Garlic Sauce
Tagliatelle of Courgette and Mangetout
Shredded Potato Pancakes

"I THINK THAT IS WONDERFUL. I LIKE EVERYTHING ABOUT THAT" LOYD

DESSERT

Caramelised Pancakes with Raspberries, Oranges and
Caramel Grand Marnier Sauce

SMOKED FISH TERRINE WITH BUTTERMERE EEL AND TWO SAUCES

3 gelatine leaves
140 ml (5 fl oz) dry white wine
200 g (7 oz) smoked salmon slices
112 g (4 oz) smoked salmon trimmings
112 ml (4 fl oz) double cream
salt and freshly ground white pepper
112 g (4 oz) smoked Buttermere eel
25 g (1 oz) sorrel leaves

Watercress and Sorrel Cream Sauce:

1 bunch of watercress, trimmed
150 ml (¼ pint) whipping cream
6 good sorrel leaves
lemon juice to taste

Horseradish Cream Sauce:

150 ml (¼ pint) whipping cream
15 ml (1 tbsp) grated fresh horseradish (see note)
30 ml (2 tbsp) lemon juice

To Garnish:

green salad leaves

Chill a small terrine or 450 g (1 lb) loaf tin in the freezer for at least 15 minutes. Soak the gelatine leaves in water to cover until soft, then squeeze out excess water. Put the gelatine leaves in a saucepan with a little of the wine and heat gently to dissolve. Mix with the remainder of the wine and allow to cool, but not set.

Pour about half of the jelly into the cold terrine and turn from side to side to give an even coating. Chill again until the jelly is set.

Line the terrine with some of the smoked salmon slices. Put the smoked salmon pieces into a food processor with half of the cream. Process for about 10 seconds, scrape down and process again until well mixed. Tip the salmon and cream mixture into a bowl and carefully mix in the rest of the cream. Season with salt and white pepper to taste. Add 45 ml (3 tbsp) of the remaining jelly and mix well.

Wrap the smoked eel fillets in sorrel leaves, then in slices of smoked salmon. Spread a third of the smoked salmon mousse in the lined terrine, lay the wrapped eel fillets on top and cover with the remaining mousse. Cover with smoked salmon slices. Pour on the remaining jelly and refrigerate for at least 1 hour.

To unmould, dip the outside of the terrine into a bowl of hot water for a few seconds, then invert onto a plate. Refrigerate until needed.

To make the watercress and sorrel cream sauce, blanch the watercress in boiling water for 30 seconds, then refresh with cold water, drain well. Purée in a blender or food processor with half of the cream, and the sorrel. Transfer to a bowl. Mix in the remaining cream, then add salt and lemon juice to taste. Refrigerate until needed.

To make the horseradish cream sauce, whisk the cream a little if necessary. Mix with the horseradish, lemon juice and salt to taste. Refrigerate until needed.

To serve, spoon a little of each sauce on to each serving plate. Slice the terrine using a warm sharp knife, into 12 mm (½ inch) slices and arrange on the plates. Garnish with green salad leaves and a little chopped jelly if desired.

Note: If fresh horseradish is difficult to obtain, simply combine a good proprietary make of creamed horseradish with double cream and seasoning to taste.

SOUTHDOWN LAMB FILLET WITH GARLIC SAUCE

600 g (1¼ lb) lamb fillet, from the loin
salt and freshly ground black pepper
14 g (½ oz) butter
4 good thyme sprigs, leaves rubbed off
  the stalks

Garlic Sauce:
20 large cloves garlic (unpeeled)
200 ml (7 fl oz) milk
20 g (¾ oz) butter
5 ml (1 tsp) sugar
500 ml (16 fl oz) good lamb or chicken stock
150 ml (¼ pint) crème fraîche

Season the lamb fillet with salt and pepper. Rub all over with the butter, then with the thyme leaves, pressing them into the meat. Leave to stand for 20 minutes or longer if possible. Place in a lightly buttered roasting tin and roast in a preheated oven at 200°C (400°F) mark 6 for 10 to 15 minutes.

To make the garlic sauce, put the garlic cloves in a saucepan and cover with the milk. Bring to the boil and cook for 1 minute; drain.

Heat the butter in a roasting tin, add the garlic, season with salt, pepper and sugar and cook over a medium heat for 2-3 minutes, stirring constantly. Transfer to the oven and bake for 15 minutes, turning the garlic frequently. Wrap 8 of the garlic cloves in foil and reserve; peel the remainder and chop finely. Place the chopped garlic in a pan with the stock and crème fraîche. Bring to the boil. Simmer until reduce to the correct consistency; you should have approximately 400 ml (14 fl oz) liquid. Pass through a sieve into a clean saucepan, pushing as much of the garlic through as possible. Adjust the seasoning.

Place the reserved garlic cloves in the oven to warm. Carve the lamb into thin slices and season with salt and pepper. Spoon a little sauce on to each plate and arrange the lamb in overlapping slices on the sauce. Spoon a little more sauce over the lamb and position two garlic cloves on each plate to garnish.

TAGLIATELLE OF COURGETTE AND MANGETOUT

125 g (4 oz) small courgettes
125 g (4 oz) mangetout
7.5 ml (½ tbsp) sesame oil

Cut the courgettes into 3 mm (⅛ inch) slices, then into thin strips. Trim the mangetout and cut lengthwise into thin strips. Mix the courgettes and mangetout together and microwave for 2 minutes, then drain. When ready to serve, heat the sesame oil in a pan, add the vegetables and mix gently to reheat.

Note: If you do not have a microwave oven, cook the courgettes and mange-tout separately in boiling salted water, allowing 1 minute for the courgettes, 1½ minutes for the mangetout. Drain well before tossing in the sesame oil.

SHREDDED POTATO PANCAKES

450 g (1 lb) potatoes, peeled
60 g (2½ oz) butter, softened
salt and freshly ground black pepper

Shred the potatoes, then squeeze to remove excess liquid and starch. Mix with half of the softened butter. Season with salt and pepper.

Heat the remaining butter in a large frying pan, divide the potato mixture into 4 portions and form into pancakes. Fry in the hot butter for about 5 minutes on each side until golden brown.

CARAMELISED PANCAKES WITH RASPBERRIES, ORANGES AND CARAMEL GRAND MARNIER SAUCE

Pancakes:
3 eggs
1.25 ml (¼ tsp) salt
5 ml (1 tsp) caster sugar
10 ml (2 tsp) grated orange rind
70 g (2¾ oz) plain flour
100 ml (3½ fl oz) double cream
60 ml (4 tbsp) milk
a little vegetable oil for frying
120 ml (8 tbsp) icing sugar
  for caramelising

Filling:
150 g (5 oz) caster sugar
400 ml (14 fl oz) fresh orange juice
3 sweet oranges
120 ml (8 tbsp) Grand Marnier
250 g (9 oz) raspberries

To Decorate:
candied orange zest julienne (see right)

To make the pancake batter, beat the eggs with the salt, sugar and grated orange rind. Stir in the flour to make a smooth batter, then stir in the cream and milk to achieve a smooth batter the thickness of double cream.

To make the sauce for the filling, dissolve the sugar in a little water in a saucepan over a low heat, then increase the heat and cook until you have a golden caramel. Carefully add the orange juice and boil until the caramel has melted and you have a clear syrupy sauce. Allow to cool.

Use the pancake batter to make 8 puffy pancakes. Heat a little oil in a crêpe pan, add an eighth of the batter and tilt to spread the batter evenly. Cook until the underside is golden, then turn and cook the other side. Repeat until all the batter is used. Stack the pancakes, interleaved with greaseproof paper as they are cooked.

Peel and segment the oranges, discarding all pith. Add to the sauce with the Grand Marnier and a third of the raspberries. Heat to just below boiling. Pour on to the remaining raspberries.

Finish the surface of each pancake by spreading evenly with the icing sugar and placing under a hot grill until the sugar has caramelised.

Place a pancake on each of 4 serving plates. Cover artistically with the fruit and sauce mixture, top with another pancake and decorate with the candied orange zest julienne.

Note: To prepare candied orange zest julienne, finely pare the rind from an orange, using a potato peeler, then cut into fine strips. Place the orange zest strips in cold water, bring to the boil and refresh with cold water. Make a syrup of equal quantities of sugar and water. Add the blanched orange strips, boil rapidly until the syrup is thick; drain.

THE FINAL

VANESSA BINNS • MARTHA SPENCER • LINDA YEWDALL

MARTHA SPENCER'S FINAL MENU

STARTER

Oyster Ravioli in a Beurre Blanc Sauce

"IF YOU KNEW THAT WAS COMING YOU WOULD NOT EAT ANOTHER RAVIOLI WOULD YOU?" CLEMENT FREUD

MAIN COURSE

Pan-fried Supremes of Quail with Grapes and a Sauternes Sauce
Seasonable Vegetables

DESSERT

Caramelised Orange and Chocolate Mousse Gâteau

"IF YOU KNEW THAT WAS COMING YOU PROBABLY WOULD NOT EAT FOR A FEW DAYS! THAT IS JUST WONDERFUL" LOYD

Oyster Ravioli in a Beurre Blanc Sauce

Pasta:
175 g (6 oz) plain flour
1 egg
60 ml (4 tbsp) water
30 ml (2 tbsp) extra virgin oil

Ravioli Filling:
20 small oysters
50 g (2 oz) butter

Sauce:
1-2 shallots, chopped
150-175 g (5-6 oz) chilled butter, diced

To Garnish:
dill sprigs

To make the pasta, sift the flour into a large bowl and make a well in the middle. Beat the egg with the water and oil, then add to the well. Incorporate the flour into the liquid ingredients, little by little. Knead the pasta for 20 minutes, then leave to rest for 30 minutes.

Meanwhile, open the oysters over a bowl to collect the juices. Strain the juice and reserve.

To make the ravioli, roll out the pasta dough thinly. Position the oysters at regular intervals over half of the dough. Dot each one with a little butter. Fold the other half of the dough over to enclose. Use a pasta wheel or other cutter to cut semi-circles around the oysters. Pinch the edges together tightly to seal.

To make the sauce, put the shallots and oyster juice in a saucepan and simmer until reduced by half. Over a low heat, beat in the butter a piece at a time. Correct the seasoning and strain.

Cook the ravioli in a large pan of boiling salted water for about 2 minutes until al dente (just tender); drain.

To serve, arrange 5 ravioli on each warmed serving plate, to resemble a flower. Pour the sauce over the ravioli, garnish with dill and serve.

PAN-FRIED SUPREMES OF QUAIL WITH GRAPES AND A SAUTERNES SAUCE

8 quail
60 ml (4 tbsp) butter
175 g (6 oz) seedless grapes, peeled
150 ml (¼ pint) sauternes wine

Croûtons:

4 slices homemade white bread, each 5 mm
  (¼ inch) thick
clarified butter for frying

Garnish:

4 slices canned 'block' foie gras, each 5 mm
  (¼ inch) thick
30 ml (2 tbsp) sauternes wine

To prepare the quail, slip your fingers between the skin and flesh, then pull away the skin. Cut against the ridge of the breastbone to loosen the flesh from the bone. Disjoint the wing where it joins the carcass and continue down along the rib cage, pulling flesh from bone as you cut until the meat from one side of the breast separates from the bone in one piece. Repeat on the other side.

To make the croûtons, cut the bread into rounds using a fluted cutter. Heat a 3 mm (⅛ inch) depth of clarified butter in a frying pan and sauté the bread rounds on each side until very lightly browned. Drain the croûtons on absorbent kitchen paper.

Place the foie gras slices in a covered dish and baste with the sauternes. Ten minutes before serving, set the dish over a pan of barely simmering water, to heat through gently.

Heat the butter in a sauté pan until it is foaming. Quickly roll the quail supremes in the butter and cook briefly until the flesh springs back with gentle resilience. Transfer the supremes to a warm platter, using a slotted spoon, and cover while making the sauce. Warm the grapes in the butter remaining in the pan, then remove with a slotted spoon. Keep warm with the supremes.

Pour the wine into the sauté pan and reduce quickly over a high heat until the liquid is syrupy. Remove from the heat and check the seasoning, then strain through a muslin-lined sieve.

To serve, arrange the quail and grapes on warmed serving plates. Pour over the sauternes sauce and garnish with the foie gras and croûtons. Serve with vegetables in season.

CARAMELISED ORANGE AND CHOCOLATE MOUSSE GÂTEAU

This sumptuous gâteau serves 6-8. I have found that Lindt chocolate gives the best result.

225 g (8 oz) plain chocolate
100 g (4 oz) unsalted butter
3 eggs, lightly beaten

Candied Orange Zest:
2 oranges
200 ml (7 fl oz) sugar syrup

Chocolate Glaze:
150 ml (¼ pint) double cream
175 g (6 oz) plain chocolate, finely chopped

To Decorate:
caramelised orange segments (optional)

Wrap the outside of a 15 cm (6 inch) springform cake tin in a double layer of foil to prevent seepage. Butter the cake tin and line the base with a round of non-stick baking parchment. Butter the paper.

To prepare the candied orange zest, finely pare long strips of zest from the oranges, using a potato peeler. Chop coarsely. Blanch in boiling water for 8 - 10 minutes, then refresh under cold water. Simmer the zest in the sugar syrup for 3 minutes, then drain.

Combine the chocolate and butter in a large heatproof bowl over a pan of hot water. Let stand, stirring occasionally, until the chocolate is melted and smooth.

Put the eggs in a large mixing bowl set over a pan of simmering water and stir constantly until warm to the touch. Remove from the heat. With an electric mixer, beat the eggs until they triple in volume and form soft peaks when the beater is lifted.

Fold half the whisked eggs into the melted chocolate until partially incorporated. Add the remaining eggs and fold in just until they are evenly blended and no streaks remain. Fold in the candied orange zest.

Pour at once into the prepared cake tin and smooth the surface with a spatula. Place in a larger roasting pan and add enough hot water to the pan to reach about two thirds of the way up the side of the cake tin.

Bake in a preheated oven at 220°C (425°F) mark 7 for 5 minutes. Cover the top of the cake tin with foil and bake for a further 10 minutes. Remove the cake tin from the roasting pan and let cool on a wire rack for 45 minutes. Then cover and refrigerate until chilled and very firm.

To make the chocolate glaze, in a small heavy-based saucepan, scald the cream. Remove from the heat and immediately add the chocolate. Stir gently until the chocolate is melted and smooth.

To unmould the cake, use a small spatula or a blunt-edged knife around the edge and remove the side of the cake tin. Carefully invert the cake onto a plate and remove the bottom of the tin. Peel off the baking parchment. Pour the tepid chocolate glaze on to the centre of the cake, letting it cascade over the side. Allow to set. Decorate the top of the cake with caramelised orange segments or leave plain if preferred.

Caramelised orange segments: Peel and segment an orange, discarding all pith. Place on a foil-lined tray and sprinkle with sugar. Caramelise with a blowtorch or under a preheated hot grill.

THE
FINAL
VANESSA BINNS • MARTHA SPENCER • LINDA YEWDALL

LINDA YEWDALL'S FINAL MENU

STARTER
Cream of Lime Soup with Coriander Croûtons

MAIN COURSE
Fillet of Beef with Cherry and Berry Sauce
Parsley Profiteroles with Horseradish Cream
Asparagus with Chive Butter
Mashed Eddoes

"THE BEEF AND HORSERADISH PROFITEROLES NEED LITTLE ELSE" RICHARD SHEPHERD

"AN INVENTION WORTH INVENTING" LOYD

DESSERT
Carrot Tart with Ginger Sauce
"GREAT LOOKING RUSTIC, HONEST PUDDING" LOYD

CREAM OF LIME SOUP WITH CORIANDER CROÛTONS

2 leeks, cleaned
2 sticks celery
25 g (1 oz) butter
2 limes
1.2 litres (2 pints) pheasant stock
2 bay leaves
salt and freshly ground black pepper
150 ml (¼ pint) single cream

Coriander Croûtons:
4 slices brown bread
50 g (2 oz) butter
5 ml (1 tsp) finely chopped coriander leaves

To Garnish:
lime slices
chives

Chop the leeks including the tops, and the celery. Melt the butter in a saucepan, add the vegetables and cook gently for 5-10 minutes until softened.

Finely pare the rind of the limes, using a potato peeler and blanch in boiling water for 1 minute. Add the blanched rind to the lime juice and leave to infuse for 5-10 minutes. Discard the rind.

To make the coriander croûtons, remove the crusts from the bread. Mix the butter with the chopped coriander and season with salt and pepper. Liberally butter the bread and put the slices one on top of the other on a piece of foil. Wrap tightly in the foil and bake in a preheated oven at 220°C (425°F) mark 7 for about 20 minutes. Check from time to time and open up the foil to crisp the croûtons.

Add the stock to the vegetables, together with the bay leaves and seasoning. Bring slowly to the boil and simmer until the vegetables are quite soft. Cool slightly, then purée in a blender or food processor.

Return the soup to a clean pan and reheat gently, stirring in the lime juice and garnish with lime slices and chives. Cut the coriander croûtons into triangles and serve with the soup.

FILLET OF BEEF WITH CHERRY AND BERRY SAUCE

700 g-1 kg (1½-2 lb) fillet of beef
about 30 ml (2 tbsp) hazelnut oil
salt and freshly ground black pepper
4-5 slices streaky bacon, derinded
125 g (4 oz) morello cherries
50 g (2 oz) sugar
squeeze of lemon juice
about 15 ml (1 tbsp) sloe gin (see right)
about 15 ml (1 tbsp) elderberry syrup
  (see below)
300 ml (½ pint) beef stock
25 g (1 oz) butter, in pieces

Brush the beef with hazelnut oil, season with salt and pepper and wrap in the bacon slices. Leave to marinate for 1 hour. Heat 15 ml (1 tbsp) hazelnut oil in a frying pan and seal the beef on all sides over a high heat. Transfer to a roasting tin and cook in a preheated oven at 220°C (425°F) mark 7 for 20 minutes or according to taste.

Meanwhile put the cherries in a saucepan with the sugar, 30-45 ml (2-3 tbsp) water and a squeeze of lemon juice. Cover and cook gently until the cherries are tender. Strain off the juice, reserving the cherries.

Transfer the beef to a warmed dish. Deglaze the roasting tin with the cherry juice, then add the sloe gin and elderberry syrup to taste. Add the stock and reduce to a sauce consistency. Stir in the butter a little at a time, then strain into a clean pan. Add the cherries to the sauce.

Carve the fillet of beef into slices and arrange on warmed plates. Pour the sauce over the meat and serve with the accompaniments.

Elderberry Syrup: Remove the stems from the elderberries, wash and drain thoroughly, then put into a saucepan. Add just enough water to cover and simmer for 30 minutes. Strain through a jelly bag or muslin into a clean pan. To each 600 ml (1 pint) add 450 g (1 lb) sugar and 10 cloves. Heat, stirring, until the sugar dissolves, then boil steadily for 10 minutes. Leave until cold, then pot in sterilized jars or bottles.

SLOE GIN

450 g (1 lb) sloes
450 g (1 lb) sugar
1 bottle of gin

Prick the sloes with a fork. Half-fill two clean dry wine bottles with the sloes. Add the sugar, top up with gin, cork and leave for at least 3 months. Decant to use.

Note: Leave the sloes in the bottle, making a tipsy trifle with the last of the fruit. Don't forget to remind your guests of the stones though!

PARSLEY PROFITEROLES WITH HORSERADISH CREAM

50 g (2 oz) butter
150 ml (¼ pint) water
65 g (2½ oz) plain flour
2 eggs, beaten
15 ml (1 tbsp) finely chopped parsley
pinch of salt

Horseradish Cream:
300 ml (½ pint) soured cream (see note)
30 ml (2 tbsp) grated fresh horseradish
salt and freshly ground black pepper

Heat the butter and water in a saucepan until the butter has melted. Bring to the boil, remove from the heat and beat in the flour to form a smooth paste. Cool slightly, then gradually add the eggs, beating all the time. Add the chopped parsley and salt.

Spoon 16 balls of dough on to a greased baking sheet. Bake in a pre-heated oven at 220°C (425°F) mark 7 for 20 minutes until golden brown and crisp. Split and pop back in the oven for a few minutes to cook the inside dough if necessary.

For the horseradish cream, mix the soured cream with the grated horse-radish and seasoning to taste. Use to fill the profiteroles.

Note: Sour double cream by adding a drop of lime juice. I always use limes in preference to lemons because a lime is a lemon with a sunny disposition!

MASHED EDDOES

350 g (12 oz) eddoes, peeled
knob of butter
dash of cream
salt
squeeze of lime juice

Quarter the eddoes, then steam until tender (or cook in boiling salted water and drain). Mash with a little butter and cream. Season with salt and a squeeze of lime juice to taste. Serve immediately.

CARROT TART WITH GINGER SAUCE

Beestings is the rich milk given by a newly calved cow. You won't get it from the shops but it's certainly worth chatting up a dairy farmer in order to get some!

Pastry:

100 g (4 oz) plain flour
50 g (2 oz) butter
15 ml (1 tbsp) icing sugar
1 small egg, size 5 or 6

Filling:

75 g (3 oz) carrot, finely grated
75 g (3 oz) brown breadcrumbs
1 whole egg, plus 1 extra yolk
150 ml (¼ pint) beestings or full-cream milk
50 g (2 oz) butter, softened
15 ml (1 tbsp) Bronte Yorkshire liqueur or brandy
10 ml (2 tsp) light muscovado sugar
¼ nutmeg, grated

Ginger Syrup:

100 g (4 oz) light muscovado sugar
300 ml (½ pint) water
5-10 ml (1-2 tsp) finely grated fresh root ginger

To Serve:

150 ml (¼ pint) Greek-style natural yogurt

Sift the flour into a bowl and rub in the butter until the mixture resembles fine breadcrumbs. Stir in the icing sugar, then add the egg to bind the pastry. Wrap and leave to rest in the refrigerator for 30 minutes.

Roll out the pastry on a lightly floured surface and use to line a 23 cm (9 inch) flan dish. Chill while making the filling.

Beat the filling ingredients together until evenly mixed. Pour into the pastry case and bake in a preheated oven at 180°C (350°F) mark 4 for 25-30 minutes until the filling has a golden crust.

Meanwhile, make the ginger syrup. Dissolve the sugar in the water in a saucepan over low heat, then increase the heat and cook until the syrup is nearly caramelised, adding ginger to taste. Allow to cool.

Dust the carrot tart with icing sugar and serve warm or cold, cut into wedges. Serve each portion with a generous spoonful of yogurt. Drizzle the ginger syrup over the yogurt.

INDEX
OF RECIPE TITLES AND CONTESTANTS